Healing & Thriving

After Domestic

Violence

A Practical Guide for Black Women

Dr. Shanita Brown

ISBN : 979-8-218-71155-9

This book is dedicated to all Black women survivors, who have endured domestic violence, *still in it*, and suffer in silence: May you find freedom from your past, strength, healing, resilience in your present, and hope for your future.

"Dr. Brown does an outstanding job weaving in her personal narrative alongside her professional experiences and research that paints a vivid, yet empowering narrative that validates the experiences of Black women, especially. I'm especially struck by her attention to intersectionality as she describes the unique nuances that Black women face."

--Dr. Joy Phifer, PhD, LCMHC, NCC, CCTP, ACS, Assistant Professor, Townsend Institute for Leadership & Consulting at Concordia University Irvine

"Healing and Thriving After Domestic Violence: A Practical Guide for Black Women" is not just a book—it's a lifeline. Grounded in lived experience, cultural awareness, and clinical knowledge, this guide provides Black women with a strong and caring road map to escape the cycle of abuse and take back their lives. Written by a Black woman survivor for Black women survivors, the book highlights voices that are far too frequently ignored and silenced. In addition to providing culturally relevant healing tools, it bravely identifies the interlocking dynamics of racism, sexism, and systemic neglect that exacerbate the trauma of domestic abuse. Every chapter speaks directly to the reader's heart and to the power of faith, community, and self-discovery. This book holds space for readers to heal at their own pace—with grace, dignity, and strength. If you are a Black woman navigating the aftermath of abuse—or walking alongside someone who is—this book is a necessary and nurturing resource. It's more than a guide. It's a declaration that Black women are worthy of peace, safety, and boundless joy.

--LaVerne H. Collins, PhD, LPC, PCMHC, NCC, Author of "Overlooked: Counselor Insights for the Unspoken Issues in Black American Life"

Dr. Shanita Brown brings an empowering, knowledgeable, and supportive message for survivors of domestic violence and those who support them in her book, *"Healing & Thriving After Domestic Violence: A Practical Guide for Black Women."* This book is based on Dr. Brown's solid professional expertise from her work as a researcher, counselor, and community advocate, along with the insights she's gained as a survivor herself. The book's message is further reinforced by highlighting the stories of other survivors who participated in Dr. Brown's research. Throughout the book, Dr. Brown offers nuanced perspectives on the cultural context surrounding domestic violence, and she offers practical wisdom on complex topics like intersectionality, systemic oppression, and the intersections of faith and culture. I'm confident this book will offer hope and inspiration to many survivors!

--Christine Murray, Ph.D, LCMHC, LMFT, Professor, and CEO of Start Here Counseling & Consulting, PLLC.

CONTENTS

Acknowledgements...ix

Introduction..xi

Why I Wrote This Book...xii

Written by One of Us, For Us...xiii

A Little About Me...xv

Book Overview..xvi

How to Use This Book...xviii

Chapter 1: What is Domestic Violence? 19

Chapter 2- Black Women's Complexities with Domestic
Violence 34

Chapter 3. Understanding Domestic Violence Trauma.......... 52

Chapter 4: We've Come This Far by Faith 69

Chapter 5: The Path to Healing: A Journey to Discovery 95

Chapter: 6. A Tribe Called Support..................................... 110

Chapter 7. Thriving After Abuse... 129

References.. 143

Resources 145

Bibliotherapy... 146

About the Author.. 147

ACKNOWLEDGEMENTS

I would like to give thanks and honor to God for entrusting me with the gift of facilitating healing. Thanks for love, strength, and grace throughout my own challenges and opportunities to excel and prepare my craft. Thank you for repurposing my pain into purpose—a beacon of hope for others. You are my ultimate guide.

To my dear clients, who for many years, have gifted me with their wounds and strengths. I am honored by your confidence in me and willingness to be vulnerable. Thanks for allowing me to partner with you and witness growth, restoration, and healing.

To my research participants, eight brave Black women, who opened up their lives and entrusted me with vivid details of your domestic violence experiences. I respect your courage to share narratives of oppression, pain, and struggle. Your stories have inspired me to write this book to empower others. You are fearless.

To Wake Chapel Church, and the HEAL Ministry; thanks for supporting "Free Not Broken" and providing a brave space for faith congregants to enhance their knowledge about domestic violence and survivors to begin their healing.

This book would not be possible without the support of family and friends. I am grateful to my mother, Cora Brown, also my momager and prayer partner. I appreciate the frequent tips of "let your work speak for itself" and "nothing is free" and constant prayers. You are my ultimate Thriver. I am grateful to Nicole Ann Hargrove, my writing accountability coach. As the title and chapters started to shape, thanks for helping me think through concepts and the encouragement to push through what ifs. "Just keep writing." To my AMCD Women Concerns Group, thanks for reaffirming my book is needed for Black women. To my second mother, the incomparable stylist—Dot Ross—thanks for your encouragement throughout this final chapter and for constantly reminding me to recognize my worth and THRIVE.

Thank you to Drs. Stephanie Helms-Pickett and Kay Reed for connecting me to my publishing team. I appreciate your support.

Many thanks to Swiner Publishing Co., and my launch team to help get this book out into the world.

INTRODUCTION

Black women deserve joy, peace, love, and a relationship free from abuse; we are unequivocally worthy of these blessings. Yet, too often, our experiences with domestic violence are overlooked, misunderstood, or minimized. When we do seek help, the systems designed to support us often fail to recognize the complexities of our experiences – our cultural identities, our history, and the ways in which racism, sexism, and systemic barriers impact our healing journey. This book was created to center Black women survivors, honor our resilience, and help us reclaim our power and our lives. Healing is not linear, and there is no one-size-fits-all approach. My hope is that this book provides you with insight, tools, and affirmation as you navigate your own journey. This book is a tribute to our strength, our survival, and our healing. It is also a call to reclaim the power that abuse tried to strip away, and to rebuild a life on our own terms – full of hope, joy, and wholeness.

WHY I WROTE THIS BOOK

I wrote this book because Black women's experiences with domestic violence are often ignored, erased, or misunderstood. We are expected to be strong, to endure, to "handle it", to "pray it away" and stay silent even when the weight of abuse is crushing us. We are less likely to be believed, more likely to be criminalized for defending ourselves, and too often left to heal in isolation.

As a Black woman survivor, I know firsthand the pain, fear, and confusion that comes with abuse. I experienced domestic violence during my undergraduate years, and at that time, I didn't have the language to name what was happening to me. I didn't have a guide that spoke to my experience, that helped me make sense of the trauma, or that affirmed my right to leave and heal.

Now, as a licensed clinical mental health counselor, researcher, and advocate, I have spent years working with survivors, and studying the impact of domestic violence on Black women. I have seen the gaps in services, the lack of culturally responsive resources, and the ways in which our healing is often overlooked. I wrote this book to fill that gap.

This book is my offering to Black women survivors. It is a space where your experiences are recognized, your pain is acknowledged, and your healing is prioritized. It combines personal narratives, research, and practical tools to help you navigate your own path forward. Whether you are still in the relationship, have left, or years into your healing, this book is for you.

Written by One of Us, For Us

This book was written by a Black woman survivor for Black women survivors. I bring to these pages my full self: survivor, counselor, scholar, and sister; combined with vulnerability and compassion. I have firsthand knowledge of how domestic violence changes you from the inside out. I know how disorienting and isolating it can feel to navigate trauma, while also trying to maintain the appearance of "having it all together". I also know the power of prayer, healing, the beauty of finding your voice, and the joy of reclaiming your life.

In addition to sharing excerpts of my own experience, I have integrated research I conducted on eight brave Black women survivors who became homeless as a result of domestic violence. Their voices, their strength, and their truths are woven throughout this guide to highlight key points and deepen your understanding. As a licensed clinical mental counselor, I also draw on my clinical experience working with Black women survivors, and my understanding of culturally specific tools and trauma-informed care. Some examples may resonate with you, and some may not, and that is okay. We are all different, but we share the common thread of surviving abuse. Take what you need on your healing journey and know that your path is valid, no matter where it begins.

I intentionally use the term survivor rather than victim to emphasize resilience, strength, and the ability to overcome abuse. While "victim" is often used within the criminal justice system, it does not fully reflect the lived experiences of those who have endured and continue to rise. Whether you are out of the relationship or still navigating your way through it – you are a survivor. You are surviving every day, and that deserves recognition and honor.

Similarly, I was deliberate in designing a book cover that resonates with Black women, focusing on imagery that reflects empowerment rather than anything triggering. You will not find images or bruised bodies or depictions of violence on this cover, because our healing journey deserves to be met with affirmation, not retraumatization. The visuals were chosen to reflect strength, beauty, and possibility because that is what I see in you – and that is what this book seeks to celebrate.

A LITTLE ABOUT ME

I am a Black woman who has lived through abuse and come out on the other side – not without scars, but with a deeper understanding of myself, my worth, and my calling. I have dedicated my career to working with survivors of domestic violence, particularly Black women who are often silenced or dismissed. My professional background includes counseling, research, and advocacy with a strong focus on uplifting the voices of Black women survivors and trauma-informed practices.

As a licensed clinical mental health counselor and supervisor, I have worked with survivors navigating the complexities of trauma, safety planning, and rebuilding their lives. As a researcher, I have studied the impact of domestic violence on Black women. My work is deeply rooted in honoring the lived experiences of Black women, challenging the systemic barriers we face, and ensuring that we have access to the resources and support we need to heal. This book is not just about my professional expertise – it is also personal. I am a survivor. I know what it means to feel trapped, to question your worth, and to wonder if healing is even possible. But I also know that freedom, joy, and wholeness are within reach. This book is my way of sharing what I have learned, both through my own journey and through the courageous women I have worked with-so that you don't have to navigate this path alone.

Book Overview

This book is structured to guide you through understanding, healing, and thriving after domestic violence. It honors your experience, your faith, your culture, and your need for practice support and encouragement. The healing strategies provided are grounded in evidence-based practices.

Chapter 1: What is Domestic Violence?

This chapter covers a foundational understanding of domestic violence such as its different forms – physical, sexual, emotional, psychological, etc. It helps you recognize the signs, patterns, and impact of abuse to gain more clarity and how it shows up in relationships.

Chapter 2: Black Women's Complexities with Domestic Violence

Here we explore the unique challenges Black women face when dealing with domestic violence, such as systemic oppression and cultural incompetency within service providers. This chapter also covers the intersection of domestic violence and our intersecting identities.

Chapter 3: Understanding Domestic Violence Trauma

Abuse leaves deep emotional and psychological wounds. This chapter helps you understand how trauma affects your brain, body, emotions, and relationships. It provides language for what you may be feeling – anxiety, numbness, shame, hypervigilance, and reassures you that your responses are valid. Understanding trauma is the first step in breaking free from its grip.

Chapter 4: We've Come This Far by Faith

This chapter honors the role of faith and spirituality in our lives. It explores how faith can be both a source of strength, and sometimes, a barrier to seeking help. It encourages you to reconnect with your faith in ways that support your healing.

Chapter 5: The Path to Healing: A Journey to Discovery

Healing is not linear, and this chapter provides tools and insights to help you navigate the emotional, mental, and physical journey of healing. It emphasizes stages of trauma recovery, barriers to healing, and healing practices that nourish your well-being.

Chapter 6: A Tribe Called Support

Healing does not happen in isolation. This chapter highlights the importance of building a support system – whether through family friends, counseling, or faith communities It offers guidance on how to find and cultivate your "tribe".

Chapter 7: Thriving After Abuse

Surviving is the first step; thriving is the goal. This final chapter explores what it means to truly thrive – reclaiming your joy, purpose, and identity. This chapter includes excerpts from survivors sharing their experiences of thriving after abuse, offering empowerment and hope for others on their healing journey.

HOW TO USE THIS BOOK

At the end of each chapter, you will find journal prompts and activities for reflection. I encourage you to take breaks when needed and incorporate a journal to capture your thoughts, emotions, and responses. Healing is a journey, and it's natural to experience a range of emotions including uncertainty about what may come up for you. These feelings are valid.

To support you as you read, I provide two key tools: deep breathing and journaling. If you feel overwhelmed, pay attention to your body and take a few deep breaths to calm and recenter yourself. Journaling can also help process emotions and gain clarity.

Honor yourself. Give yourself permission to take your time, to feel, and to heal at your own pace. This book is not just about surviving – it's about reclaiming your power, your peace, and your future. I believe in you; I am with you. So, let's get started.

CHAPTER 1: WHAT IS DOMESTIC VIOLENCE?

"A healthy relationship would be nice for me in the future."

--Janet Jackson

"Hey sis! Do the following statements sound familiar?

"Gurl, we are often up and down; or this is just our love language?"

"...He's not really yelling... just talks loud... you know it's just how we do," or maybe this...

"At times, I feel like I'm walking on eggshells... but I love him and believe this is just a phase. It won't happen again."

"It's not that bad because he's not hitting me."

Nine times out of ten, you have heard or said these statements or described other relationships. In a similar way, your experiences have influenced your subconscious mind, resulting in repeated self-dialogue questioning if what you are experiencing is love, abuse, a situationship, entanglement, or a phase. First things first, you are not ALONE, and you're not crazy. Second, I've engaged in this internal conflict and have often heard this from my clients and research participants. Third, relationships are not always easy, and depending upon what relationships you saw growing up, you may not be able to determine what is healthy, unhealthy, or abusive. Last, and most importantly, YOU deserve a loving, healthy, respectful relationship. So, let's get into this.

One in four women will experience some form of intimate partner violence (domestic violence, sexual assault, stalking, or rape) in their lifetime. According to the National Intimate Partner Violence Survey (2016), approximately 44 % of Black women have experienced domestic violence compared to

34.6% of White women and 2.5 times the rate of women of other races. But why are Black women experiencing domestic violence at higher rates? My research aligns with previous studies conducted on reasons for the high occurrences of domestic violence for Black women. What I found is that historical oppression and present-day racism, the role of faith/spirituality, negative stereotypes, the vulnerability of Black men to police brutality, and loyalty to our community are contributing factors to why Black women experience domestic violence at higher rates than their counterparts.

The reality is that many Black women suffer in love; we have a long history of equating pain with love. Sometimes, we believe that pain is a pathway to love. Why? There is this notion that Black women are durable enough to endure emotional, physical, and psychological labor dating back to slavery: that STRONG Black Woman. Also, we've witnessed mamma n em' take a lot of crap to stay married, and because of this, we somehow believe that chaos, yelling, intimidation, manipulation, and so forth are normal. However, that is far from the truth, and it doesn't have to be this way. Therefore, it is critical to educate yourself about abusive relationships so that you are empowered to make an informed decision about whether to stay or leave the relationship.

Also, because of the stigma and shame surrounding domestic violence, our stories often go untold, and many of us suffer in silence. I've noticed that a lot of Black women hesitate to recognize or admit they're in abusive relationships—and I understand why. For years, shame and stigma kept me quiet too. I didn't tell anyone what I had been through. I mean, who walks around saying, "I've experienced domestic violence." It took time for me to process everything, to realize it wasn't my fault, and to reclaim my voice. So, please, don't carry shame—you're not alone. Truth be told, the shame and stigma belong to the abuser. You didn't do anything wrong; it wasn't your fault. They violated you.

Plus, depending on the severity and duration of domestic

violence, it can take years to fully come to terms with what you have been through. This is normal, especially when the trauma runs deep and the violence has been long lasting—a repetitive, toxic cycle. To add to that, one of the most confusing aspects of an abusive relationship is that certain parts can appear healthy or even feel loving. For example, an abuser might be supportive in your career or show affection in public, creating moments that feel genuine and nurturing. There may be laughter, shared goals, or times of peace that resemble a healthy connection. These moments can make it harder to recognize the relationship as abusive, especially when they're mixed with manipulation, control, or harm. This duality—the presence of both care and cruelty—can keep you in a cycle of hope and confusion. It's important to understand that even if some aspects feel positive, they don't cancel out the abuse. Healthy relationships don't require you to tolerate harm in exchange for love. So don't beat yourself up for not knowing what you didn't know before. Instead, apply self-compassion for where you are and the steps you have taken to learn more about the dynamics of abuse. Knowledge is a powerful tool for healing and growth. Reading this book is an empowering step toward deepening your understanding of abusive relationships and equipping yourself for the future.

In this chapter, we will cover some basic concepts about abusive relationships because this is still a taboo subject in the Black community; many don't know what is healthy or abusive. Also, increasing awareness helps you make an informed decision about whether to stay or leave, and you're more equipped to protect yourself and others moving forward. To highlight the prevalence of misinformation or lack of information about domestic violence, I want to introduce you to the voices of eight Black women survivors who participated in my research. Each of these women experienced homelessness as a result of domestic violence. Their ages ranged from 25–55, and they came from a variety of backgrounds, having grown up in rural, suburban, and urban communities. Their educational experiences spanned from earning a GED to completing a master's degree. At the time of the interviews, some were employed while others were not. Some had children—ranging in age from 11 months to 10 years old—while others did not.

Two were preacher kids, or "PK" kids, meaning their parents were faith leaders, adding an important layer to how they made sense of their experiences. Their histories of domestic violence lasted anywhere from two and a half to twenty years, with an average duration of eight years. To protect their identities, I have used pseudonyms: Rachel, Carla, April, Bobbi, Vanessa, Sami, Sarah, and Tina. The quotes that follow reflect their personal understandings of domestic violence and offer insight into the ways misinformation, silence, and survival shaped their journeys.

"My boyfriend was nice, loving, and caring in the beginning of our relationship. However, I noticed some changes that concerned me; he became more insecure and limited my time with family and friends. So, I began looking into abuse online and tried to educate myself. If there is somebody in a domestic violence relationship, and see early signs and red flags, leave, because it's a blessing to make it out." —Bobbi

"When someone is mean to you and they say they love you, but they don't, and they take advantage of you, your kindness for your weakness, and once they've got you at your weakest point is when they feel like they're in control of you. They have all the control, and they can do anything they want to you and think that they can get away with it. I really don't know; trying to figure it out." —Tina

"You're always fighting and arguing; never trying to talk to each other or explain things; never listening to each other; just so much assuming and arguing." —Carla

"I didn't think emotional abuse was actually domestic violence, but the first time that I realized that I was in an abusive relationship was when it got physical. Because I think I defined domestic violence as physical; it had to be continually physical in order for it to be a domestic violence situation. I think this

22

showed me that there were so many dynamics to domestic violence than I ever knew." —Sara

Recognizing Red Flags

As you can see, the participants didn't recognize they were in an abusive relationship. I didn't either. Abusers are manipulative, and they rarely present as abusive at the start of a relationship; they often appear charming, attentive, and loving, which can make the early stages feel safe and even ideal. This initial warmth can mask controlling behaviors that gradually intensify over time, making it harder to recognize the abuse as it unfolds. Abuse doesn't always start with physical violence. More often, it begins with subtle forms of control and manipulation that gradually escalate over time. Many survivors recall early warning signs—red flags, but at the time, you may have dismissed them as normal relationship issues or even mistaken them for love. For example, abusers may shower you with excessive attention and affection early on (called love bombing) to create emotional dependency. They might become overly jealous or possessive, claiming it's because they care. Over time, this can turn into controlling behaviors, such as monitoring your phone, dictating what you wear, or deciding who you can and cannot spend time with. Also, small criticisms may escalate into verbal put-downs, designed to chip away at your confidence and make you doubt your worth.

Another major red flag is isolation—an abuser may try to separate you from friends, family, or anyone who could recognize the behavior and support you. They might make you feel guilty for wanting to spend time with others or create conflict to drive a wedge between you and your loved ones. Financial control, threats, unpredictable mood swings, and making you feel responsible for their emotions or actions are all warning signs of an unhealthy and potentially dangerous relationship. Some of the red flags I experienced include manipulation, subtle jabs, and overwhelming attention that didn't feel as loving as it appeared. For instance, he insisted on picking me up from class so I wouldn't have to ride the university bus—what seemed thoughtful at first. But later, he used that "favor" to justify controlling when and where I spent time with my friends. I remember one of my older sisters pulling me aside and saying she thought some of his behavior seemed excessive, and she wasn't sure she trusted his intentions. Looking back, she saw what I couldn't yet name. In summary, recognizing these red flags is key to protecting yourself because love should never feel like fear, control, or confusion. As you think of your experience, are any of these red flags familiar? Take a moment to reflect and jot down your response for the upcoming activity.

I have provided various forms of abuse and key terms below:

Intimate Partner Violence: An umbrella term used to describe physical, sexual, or psychological harm by a current or former partner and spouse (Center for Disease Control, 2018).

Domestic Violence: Pattern of coercive and assaultive behaviors by one partner to gain power and control over their partner. For the purpose of this book, this term is used to encompass the range of physical, psychological, verbal, and spiritual abuse by survivors at the hands of their partners. This term is most popular in the Black community and will be used rather than intimate partner violence.

Oppression/Systems of Oppression: When a person or group of people have power and use it in a way that is unjust, harmful, and discriminatory to underserved and marginalized people and communities. In the context of this book, systems of oppressions are systemic barriers that Black women experience while enduring domestic violence. Examples include racism, sexism, classism, and ableism.

Patriarchy/Patriarchal Violence: A system of social practices and structures in which men govern, oppress, and exploit women. Patriarchal violence is any type of violence to maintain or create male power; this can range from verbal, physical, psychological, financial to sexual violence.

Sexual Violence: Encompasses sexual assault, rape, sexual abuse, child sexual abuse, and molestation in which a person forces another individual to engage in a sexual act without consent or against their will.

Physical Abuse: Involves a person utilizing physical force against another person to cause harm. Examples include but are not limited to slapping, hitting, punching, biting, choking, kicking, using weapons or other acts that hurt or threaten. It usually starts out with a slap or hit and gradually intensifies over time.

Emotional/Psychological Abuse: Includes but not limited to criticism, demeaning comments, name-calling, undervaluing a victim's self-esteem or self-worth, intimidation, and forcing isolation from family, friends, and activities.

Stalking: A pattern of unwanted behavior that involves repeatedly following or contacting a person, monitoring, and harassment.

Cyberstalking: Repeated use of electronic communication, like the internet or cell phones, to harass or frighten someone.

Spiritual Abuse: Misuse of religion and spirituality to maintain power and control over another partner. For example, utilizing religious scriptures, cultural and familial teachings and traditions, spiritual beliefs to manipulate, guilt, or shame another partner. Or forcing someone to violate their religious practices. Also, it can be a person in a position of spiritual authority, such as a pastor, bishop, or elder that abuses their position to control members. Spiritual abuse is not limited to a certain denomination or religion.

Gaslighting: Psychological manipulation that causes you to question yourself, beliefs, and perception of reality.

Financial Abuse: Occurs in about 99% of domestic violence cases, also known as the silent weapon. It can be subtle or overt, and involves the abuser utilizing tactics to hide information, limit the victim's access to bank accounts, and other family finances. In some cases, financial abuse will become present once the victim decides to leave or has left the relationship.

Knowledge is power, and understanding the basics about abusive relationships is empowering as you gain self-awareness and obtain confidence for your healing journey. One of the first tools I have found to be highly effective with clients in examining their abusive relationships is the Power and Control Wheel. This resource, created in the early 80s, is utilized in the domestic violence field to help survivors understand one of the most important elements of abusive relationships: a variety of tactics abusers utilize to gain power and control over another person. Each segment of the wheel represents a controlling tactic to maintain power and control. I utilized this tool in the early stages of therapy as many survivors have a difficult time identifying their experiences as abuse, especially if it's emotional abuse. Also, being that the majority of Black women initially seek guidance for domestic violence from their faith leader many have never seen or heard of the Power and Control Wheel. For survivors that have sought assistance from a domestic violence agency, most likely you've seen it. For people outside the domestic violence field, you probably haven't either. You can find the wheel at https://www.theduluthmodel.org Also, I have provided it on the next page.

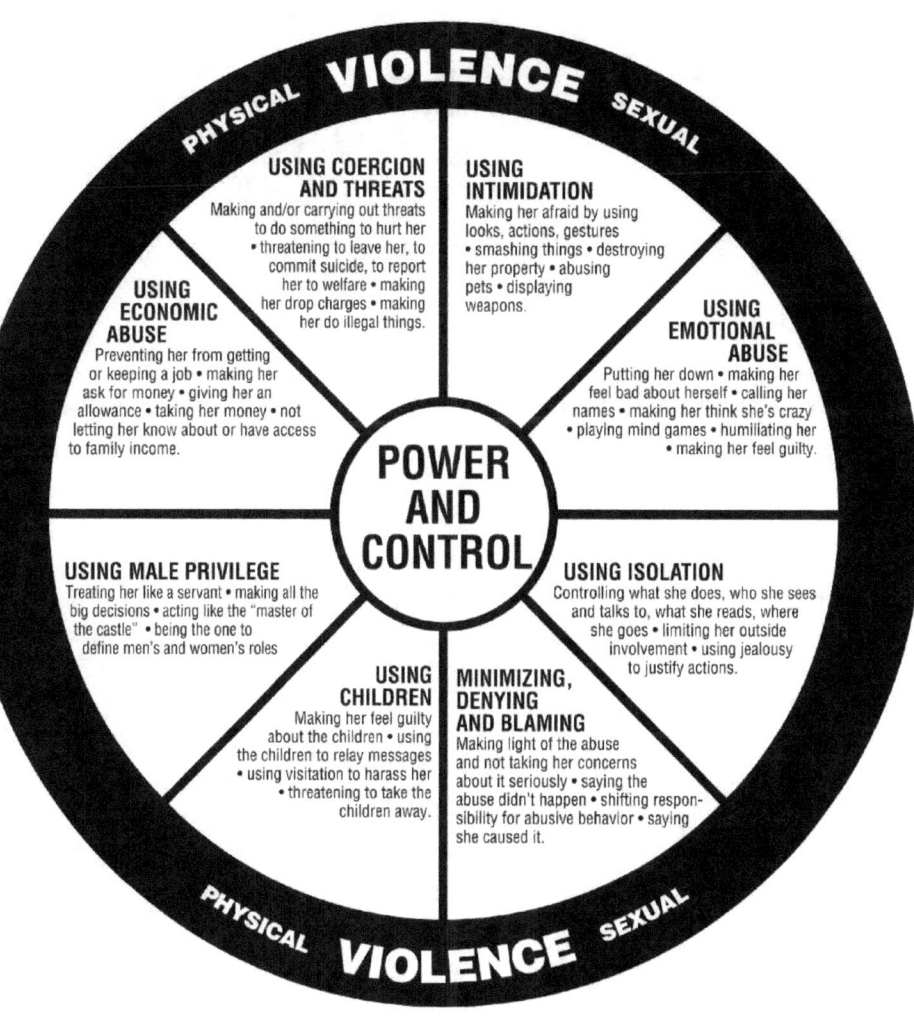

POWER AND CONTROL

USING COERCION AND THREATS
Making and/or carrying out threats to do something to hurt her • threatening to leave her, to commit suicide, to report her to welfare • making her drop charges • making her do illegal things.

USING INTIMIDATION
Making her afraid by using looks, actions, gestures • smashing things • destroying her property • abusing pets • displaying weapons.

USING EMOTIONAL ABUSE
Putting her down • making her feel bad about herself • calling her names • making her think she's crazy • playing mind games • humiliating her • making her feel guilty.

USING ECONOMIC ABUSE
Preventing her from getting or keeping a job • making her ask for money • giving her an allowance • taking her money • not letting her know about or have access to family income.

USING MALE PRIVILEGE
Treating her like a servant • making all the big decisions • acting like the "master of the castle" • being the one to define men's and women's roles

USING ISOLATION
Controlling what she does, who she sees and talks to, what she reads, where she goes • limiting her outside involvement • using jealousy to justify actions.

USING CHILDREN
Making her feel guilty about the children • using the children to relay messages • using visitation to harass her • threatening to take the children away.

MINIMIZING, DENYING AND BLAMING
Making light of the abuse and not taking her concerns about it seriously • saying the abuse didn't happen • shifting responsibility for abusive behavior • saying she caused it.

PHYSICAL **VIOLENCE** SEXUAL

DOMESTIC ABUSE INTERVENTION PROGRAMS
202 East Superior Street
Duluth, Minnesota 55802
218-722-2781
www.theduluthmodel.org

Activity 1

1. Review the power and control wheel and reflect on your relationship. What resonates with you? What stands out for you? What role does familial upbringing and culture play into these experiences? Use this space to write down your feelings and thoughts.

Cycle of Violence

The cycle of violence theory is another important concept. Developed by Dr. Lenore Walker, this cycle refers to four distinct phases often found in abusive relationships that keep survivors trapped in an abusive vicious cycle. It helps explain the complexity and cohabitation of love and abuse. The cycle is also known as the cycle of abuse because it describes the cyclical behavior patterns of abusers, its impacts on you, and provides insight on why you stayed longer or are still in the relationship. For example, research indicates it takes an average of seven attempts for survivors to permanently leave an abusive relationship. This is due to several factors such as financial dependence, attachment, hope, fear, and the cycle of abuse. Thus, this aspect of abusive relationships is helpful to not only professionals but also for everyday people seeking to better understand this repetitive cycle of chaos, confusion, and turbulence.

I also found this resource helpful during my healing journey and for clients, because 1) We do not recognize we are in a cycle, blinded by abuse, masked by a person that we thought was loving, but really did not exist. 2) We are deeply holding on and hoping for change. The loving tender moments we experience in the relationship, combined with repeated abusive moments, leaves you confused and stuck. As a result, any plans or thoughts to leave are canceled or delayed. Instead, we hold on to those moments because it provides a sense of optimism; a yearning that things will continue in a consistent positive direction. However, the only thing constant is the cycle of violence. Let's further discuss the cycle:

1. Tension Building Phase - the first phase in the cycle. The abuser is quick-tempered, irritable, uncommunicative, and frustrated due to stressors such as issues at work, economic conditions, and family problems. For someone in this stage, this feels like you are walking on eggshells, feeling as if something is about to happen, always worrying about "what ifs," or you are trying to keep the peace – appease or pacify the abuser to avoid an explosive or violent incident. For instance, Rachel shared, *"It was a struggle everyday to wake up and be scared of somebody not knowing what mood he would be in or what to expect."*

2. Incident/Violent Episode Phase - the second phase in the cycle. The abuser is violent either physically, sexually, or verbally. They may destroy property or turn minor disagreements into an explosive argument. For someone in this stage, you may be beaten, raped or physically attacked for no apparent reason, or you may experience constant fear for your life or children's safety. For instance, Bobbi shared, *"It started out good and then it got bad. He was very insecure and very, very controlling. Then, when I did let him control me, he would get upset. It was bad. I could be sitting here, and he could be sitting there, and if he feels I'm doing something for no reason, he would throw something at me or get up and come over and push me outdoors, take my car keys, just anything."* During this phase, you recognize there is a relationship problem but are unsure what to do or how to fix it. You feel the abuse is your fault.

3. Reconciliation Phase - the third phase. The abuser is very apologetic, extremely loving, remorseful, and kind. They may buy flowers, gifts, promises to stop drinking, gambling, using drugs, seeing other women, hanging out, and other things they feel is responsible for their violent behavior. Also, the abuser blames you, and may deny, minimize the abuse, or gaslight you into questioning if what you experience was actually abuse.

29

Abusers are clever, always finding ways to keep you trapped; they want to change your perception of what happened to maintain power and control. Sounds like *awwww... I'm sorry... it will never happen again, I love you, I'll get help, remember why we fell in love*. For someone in this stage, you really believe these promises because you want to avoid any additional physical or emotional attacks and/or desire to keep a loving relationship. Also, when you receive flowers, gifts, and spend more time together, chemicals in the brain such as oxytocin and dopamine are released, so you feel warm and fuzzy. The bonding boosts affection, combined with hope and optimism that the relationship will work itself out. In other words, the violent phase was just a phase. For instance, my abuser repeatedly apologized and offered nice dinners, trips, concerts, etc. I thought he was remorseful, but this "forgiveness" phase slowly disappeared. I found myself on pins and needles again, unaware I was reentering the tension-building phase – this vicious cycle of entrapment.

4. Calm/Honeymoon Phase - the fourth phase. During this phase, everything in the relationship is pretty much peaceful; no complaints - peachy keen. The abuser is still apologetic, on their best behavior, and you all may discuss what happened. In other words, you are seeking an explanation, only to be told if you had not done something, you wouldn't have experienced harm. It was your fault. For someone in this stage, you may have forgotten what happened because the abuser is very clever and manipulates you into believing the incident was trivial. In addition, you may still have mixed feelings of love, care, and affection for an abuser, and often make excuses for them. To add to that, you and the abuser may totally forget about the previous incident and carry on as if nothing happened. Or you may think leaving during the calming stage is okay, but due to a pattern of controlling tactics, you are afraid.

Yet, the calm phase will eventually pass, as tension in the relationship escalates and the cycle starts all over again. For me, this phase was challenging because when I felt everything was "good," I honestly thought it was over. I did not understand that while there weren't any active physical or explosive incidents, the abuse was still there. When abuse is dormant, it is very hard to recognize invisible wounds. So, we continue to suffer through emotional wars since we are not physically battered and bruised.

In closing, the cycle of violence model is a frequently utilized theory in domestic violence education. Understanding the cycle of violence can be an illuminating experience for anyone that has experienced domestic violence and anyone currently in an abusive relationship. Quite often people are surprised how closely the models reflect their experiences and are now able to view their experiences from a new lens. Also, clarity about this vicious cycle is critical to your freedom from abuse, serves as a source of empowerment, and lets you know that you are not alone. Keep in mind not everyone will experience all the phases, and abuse is very unpredictable. The phases can all happen in one day, weeks, or months; it is different for every relationship. Domestic violence is very complex, and there are various forms of it. It is hard to cover every aspect in this chapter, but I aimed to review the foundational aspects of abusive relationships. It is my hope from this chapter that your experiences have been validated, and you are more informed about domestic violence. With knowledge, awareness, and supportive appropriate interventions, the cycle of violence can be broken. You do not have to live in a cycle of fear on a daily basis. You have a choice; I encourage you to choose YOU. Remember, you did **NOT** cause the abuse. Abuse is **NEVER** your fault. Domestic violence is a **CHOICE**, and the abuser **HAS** to make a decision to change their behavior; you cannot change them. The cycle of violence is the abuser's cycle, you are feeling the impact. However, if you're still on the fence about your relationship or whether what you are experiencing is abuse, it is okay. Coming to terms with what you are experiencing is a process. It was a process for me. To support your understanding, I have included an infographic illustrating the cycle of violence on the next page.

Activity 2: Review the Cycle of Violence Infographic

Cycle of Abuse

1 Tensions Building
Tensions increase, breakdown of communication, victim becomes fearful and feels the need to placate the abuser

4 Calm
Incident is "forgotten", no abuse is taking place. The "honeymoon" phase

2 Incident
Verbal, emotional & physical abuse Anger, blaming, arguing. Threats. Intimidation.

3 Reconciliation
Abuser apologizes, gives excuses, blames the victim, denies the abuse occured, or says that it wasn't as bad as the victim claims

1. If you are currently in an abusive relationship, what phase represents your relationship? What steps can you take to break the cycle of violence? If you do not feel safe, please call 911, or the DV hotline at 1-800-799-SAFE.

2. If you are not in an abusive relationship, what phase/phases have you experienced? What feelings are surfacing?

Reflection Prompt

1. Jot down any messages or thoughts that came up for you after reading this chapter.

2. What is something new that you have learned about domestic violence?

3. How has your previous knowledge about domestic violence shifted?

4. Have you ever ignored or rationalized harmful behavior? Why?

5. What is your biggest takeaway from this chapter and how will you utilize this information?

Chapter 2- Black Women's Complexities with Domestic Violence

"There is no such thing as a single-issue struggle because we don't live single-issue lives." —Audre Lorde

When I reflect on the word "complexities," my mind often wanders to the word "complexion." It seems like a weird association. But when I think about complexities and then complexion, it makes me think back to the days when I, like many other Black women, struggled with knowing which colors complemented my skin tone. Life took on an added layer of complexity when I realized there was a relationship between the color of my clothes and the tones of my complexion. Realizing that relationship also made me realize this: As Black women, our whole existence is complex. Our identities are multifaceted or layered and composed of so many parts and elements that all intertwine to form who we are.

This reality leads to the point of this chapter: the complicated web of connections between Black women and domestic violence and its impact on us. The subject matter at hand is not for the weak; it is layered, thick, and intricately woven. In fact, it's "thicker than a Snicker," as the saying goes. However, in order to move forward - both within the pages of this book and within society at large - we must first unravel these layers and painstakingly untangle the threads that bind Black women's experiences with domestic violence.

We as Black women don't have single issues struggles; instead, we face unique, layered, and complex challenges, and it is caused by some of our primary identities such as race, gender, economic status, religion, and sexual orientation. These overlapping identities mean we often experience multiple layers of oppression. Research shows that Black women dealing with abusive relationships face several obstacles. I am here to give you more than the tea; you will read real-life examples of the complexities. No, you're not crazy for feeling how you feel. It's REAL out here.

To understand the topics ahead, I have to break down the complexities tied to Black women's experiences with domestic violence. This means we have to examine the intersecting identities and systemic factors that shape our experiences. The impact of factors such as socioeconomic status to cultural incompetency and racial societal stress on our intersecting identities cannot be overlooked. Moreover, gender and sexual orientation, and the inaccessibility of professional services further complicate the challenges faced by Black women confronting domestic violence.

I have to put my therapist's voice back on for this part. The whole idea of **intersectionality** was introduced by feminist theorist and legal scholar Kimberlé Crenshaw in 1995. She created the concept to criticize feminists and frameworks that often overlooked the experiences of individuals who faced multiple forms of discrimination. For example, those who watered down the connection between gender and domestic violence. See, intersectionality looks at how different social identities, like race, gender, and class, intersect and impact the lives of marginalized people (us) all at once. It shows how systems of oppression, such as racism and sexism, combine and overlap to create complex forms of discrimination. When you understand intersectionality, you see that the domestic violence experiences of Black women are legit. By you and others acknowledging the multiple identities a Black woman has in abusive relationships, voices and perspectives that are often silenced and misunderstood can be highlighted. Acknowledging intersectionality for yourself is essential because it helps to reveal and confirm how systemic injustice and social inequality occur on different levels and how Black women remain in a marginalized and oppressed position.

In essence, the journey ahead is tense with complexities, but it is also filled with stories of resilience and possibility. By peeling back the layers and confronting the realities of Black women's encounters with domestic violence, we can pave the way for meaningful change and liberation. This chapter covers the unique challenges Black women encounter in the context of domestic violence, including systemic oppression, and delves into how our intersecting identities shape these experiences.

Systemic Oppression

This piece of the pie is a little harder to see, like that invisible lace, but it's there! I am going to explain how structural inequalities and systemic injustices intersect with domestic violence, particularly for Black women. First off, it's crucial to understand that the systems in place - the legal system, healthcare system, and social services - are not always on our side. Discriminatory practices within these systems can make it even harder for us Black women to get the help we need when experiencing abuse. It's like the deck is stacked against us from the start.

Okay, professional voice again. Here's the quick tea on one way therapists like myself view the world when we are trying to understand oppression on multiple levels. We use Critical Race Theory (CRT) and you can too. This framework helps everyone understand how our barriers are not just random –they're part of a larger system of institutional racism and systemic barriers that limit resources for Black women who are trying to leave abusive relationships. It's like shining a light on the ways in which the system is rigged against us, keeping us trapped in cycles of abuse.

Imagine you're a Black woman trying to escape an abusive relationship. You're reaching out for support, but everywhere you turn, there's a barrier in your way. Maybe it's because you live in a neighborhood where there are no shelters nearby, or maybe it's because you don't have the money to pay for counseling or legal assistance. Whatever the reason, it's clear that the system is failing.

Structural inequalities and systemic injustices intersect with domestic violence. They shape the resources and support available to Black women. Discriminatory practices within legal, healthcare, and social service systems may further marginalize survivors. Structural and institutional racism also contribute significantly to economic inequality, often blaming those at the bottom of the socioeconomic ladder for their situations. Black women are disproportionately affected by poverty; while they make up 6% of the U.S. population, they account for nearly 37% of females from impoverished backgrounds. They represent one of the largest groups of women living in poverty.

All of the women mentioned throughout these pages fit right in this section too. Each woman recalls a time when they have felt discriminated against, blamed, targeted, or overlooked by the systems there to provide service and help.

See, it's not just about race, or gender, or class—it's about how all these things intersect and compound each other. When we talk about systemic injustice and social inequality, we have to look at the bigger picture. We have to understand how Black women are facing multiple layers of oppression and how that keeps us trapped in a marginalized and oppressed position. The Multicultural Power & Control Wheel in Activity 3 is a powerful tool you can use to understand the layers. I find it helpful for acknowledging the unique cultural, historical, and systemic factors that shape Black women's experiences with domestic violence. I also find it validates and instills hope in their healing journey. The Multicultural Power & Control Wheel (Activity 3) is an extension of the original Power & Control Wheel (Activity 1). It was designed to highlight how intersecting identities (race/ethnicity, gender, sexual orientation, ableism, religion, disability, socioeconomic status, and age) shape the domestic violence experiences of Black and brown women. (Chavis & Hill, 2009). I have provided the

Multicultural Power and Control Wheel and invite you to reflect on your experiences with it. Have you ever felt like your race, culture, or background was used against you in your relationship or when you sought assistance? What did that feel like? Take a moment to reflect and journal your responses. This exercise is meant to help you recognize and name experiences that may have been minimized, misunderstood, or dismissed—especially when cultural identity intersects with abuse. Honor whatever comes up for you in this process.

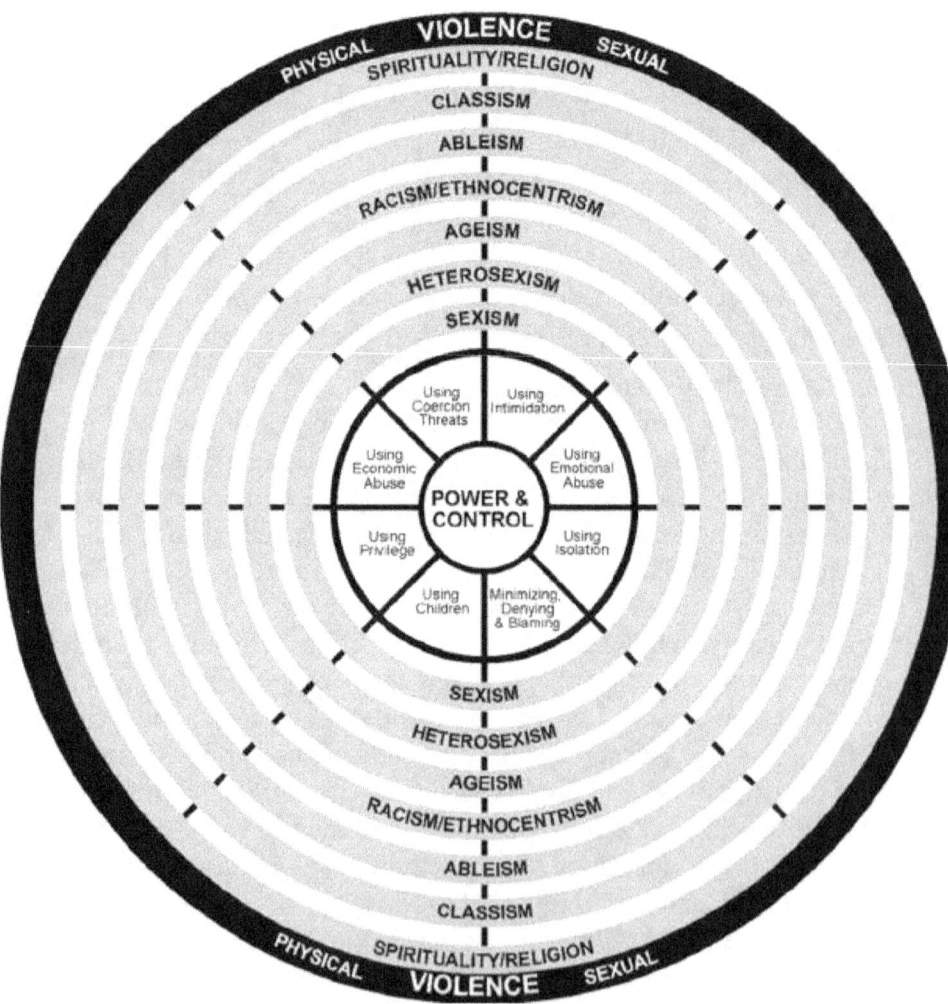

The Impact of Intersecting Identities

Okay, I have to use my professional voice for this part too. Like I said before, the impact of intersecting identities on Black women's experiences with domestic violence is profound and multilayered. These intersecting identities such as race/ethnicity, gender, sexual orientation, age, religion/spirituality, disability, and socioeconomic status, create overlapping layers of oppression, disadvantage, and vulnerability. This means our challenges are intensified when in abusive situations. I repeat: acknowledging [the nature of these overlapping connections] is [necessary] because it helps to bring light to how systemic injustice and social inequality occur on a multidimensional basis and how Black women remain in a marginalized and oppressed position.

Alright, let's break this down in plain English. You've got all these different parts of who you are, right? Like, your job, your habits, your background, and stuff like that. Now, imagine those parts all mixing together, kind of like a big ol' gumbo. That's what I mean when I talk about "intersecting identities." Now, when you throw in things like how much money you've got, whether you're dealing with substance use, or how society sees you based on your race or gender, it gets even more complicated. Like, those parts of who you start overlapping and getting all tangled up together like a cheap wig. And for Black women, it's like trying to untangle a mess of headphones - you just keep running into more knots. Here's the thing: all these overlapping parts of who we are, they don't just sit there quietly. Nope, they actually make life a whole lot tougher, especially when we're dealing with domestic violence. It's like adding extra weight to an already heavy load.

Understanding how all these different parts of your life mix together is super important. It's like turning on a light in a dark room - it helps you see how unfair things are and why Black women often get stuck in these tough situations. Now, let's dig into the impact of each identity. As we dig into each one, we're going to continue to step into the lives of Rachel, Carla, April,

Bobbi, Vanessa, Sami, Sarah, and Tina. Real women with real stories to tell. It's about to go down.

Every survivor's story will be different and the same. It seems like we are genetically disposed to share similar life experiences, but the situations and processes that bring us to those points are different. So, even if you are not a Black woman who has been dealt the hand of poverty or slipped into substance abuse, you are still tangled in the complexities.

Socioeconomic Status aka Poverty

You know how life throws some curveballs, right? Well, for us Black women, one of those curveballs can be poverty. It's like we're carrying the weight of the world on our shoulders, but society keeps piling on more. Here's the deal: even though we make up just a small chunk of the population, we're holding down a big chunk of the poverty stats. Like, seriously, nearly 37% of the sisters living in poverty are us. It's not just about scraping by - it's about struggling to survive. Not to mention income inequality hits Black women especially hard. If you live in poverty-stricken neighborhoods, unfortunately, you'll experience higher rates of domestic violence compared to women on the other side of town (Hetling & Zhang, 2010). Poor Black women are just more vulnerable to domestic violence due to their lower socioeconomic status. With limited economic opportunities and inadequate social support systems, they often feel trapped in relationships, and those relationships tend to be abusive.

With that being said, that puts me in mind of Bobbi. Bobbi is a 25-year-old mother of three children. During the time of our interview, she was employed full-time, approximately 45 minutes away from the shelter. As Bobbi reflected on the dynamics of the relationship with her partner, she acknowledged that things were once good. She described her partner as nice, caring, and loving on one occasion. However, as the relationship advanced, she noticed changes in his

40

behavior that raised some concerns. She said that her partner had become very insecure and controlling and had victimized her on multiple occasions. Unfortunately, although she was still very young, Bobbi had endured a substantial amount of physical and emotional abuse. Bobbi pointed out that when she first attempted to find assistance for domestic violence, she was told that her income level was too high. Yes, I made the same face too.

Now, picture this: you're trying to make ends meet, dealing with bills, worrying about your health, and all that stuff. And then, on top of all that stress, you're stuck in an abusive relationship. It's like being trapped in a nightmare, but your Freddy is someone you love, and you can't wake up. The thing is, when you're stuck in poverty, it's harder to break free from an abusive situation. You don't have as many options, and the support systems that should have your back? Yeah, ghosted! They're not always there when you need them. So, it's no surprise that dealing with all this mess can mess with your head, right? Feeling worthless, hopeless, like there's no way out - it's a heavy load to carry. Bobbi shared this reality.

On one occasion, due to lack of transportation and housing, she couldn't go to social services to reinstate her children's Medicaid. I know now much of that is done online, but even with that, there are still some families who do not have access to the internet and a computer. And like Bobbi, at times they don't have the transportation to make it to a location with internet and computers.

"When I told the social worker my domestic violence story that led to no transportation and housing. . . I was denied Medicaid and told. . . not to take the system for granted." —Bobbi

Despite it all, there's a silver lining: we're stronger than we think. Life throws a lot of crap our way, but we've got resilience and faith running through our veins. And together, we continue to rise above the struggle, find our strength, and break free from the chains that bind us. The chapters ahead will help you dive deeper, shine a light on the battles you've fought, and map out the path to freedom. So, grab a seat and cup, and let's journey together toward healing, empowerment, and a brighter tomorrow.

Cultural Incompetency

Cultural insensitivity within institutions and service providers creates barriers that can prevent Black women from accessing appropriate and effective support. The struggle to find support when you need it most is sometimes bootleg and shady. See, when it comes to dealing with domestic violence, the last thing you need is another barrier by being revictimized. Unfortunately, that's exactly what many of us faced when we tried to reach out for help.

Vanessa's experience fits this to the T. Vanessa, a 55-year-old former teacher and mother of five children and six grandchildren, grew up witnessing domestic violence between her mother and father and credited this volatile environment as the beginning of her domestic violence cycle. When asked about her experience accessing resources, Vanessa explained she was aware of the perceptions White people could have about Black women on welfare. Still, she did not want her children to grow up in the violent environment as she had, so she told me about the time she went to social services to improve the living situation for her and her children.

"I am not lazy or a 'welfare queen' trying to live off the system... I really need help." Vanessa recounted details about her experiences with hostility and prejudice: "Standing with tears in my eye, the social worker said... you people always need help... I'm sorry we can't help you at this time... have you tried the churches?" —Vanessa

We have been historically stereotyped as "welfare queens." Tuh! This further discourages Black women from seeking assistance because we just know someone is going to have us bent like elbows and twisted like a pretzel. Who wants to willingly be labeled and treated unfairly? This combination of economic hardship and societal prejudice creates a complex barrier for Black women trying to escape abusive situations.

Picture this reality: you're hurting, scared, and desperate for someone to understand. But when you finally get up the courage to seek support, you're met with blank stares, language barriers, and judgments that cut deep. You're revictimized and it's like pouring salt on an open wound, making the pain even worse.

It's beyond sad that the very places that are supposed to help us, like domestic violence agencies, often fall short when it comes to understanding our unique experiences. They might mean well, but without cultural competency skills and training, they end up missing the mark and causing even more harm by revictimizing Black women. And let's not forget about the stereotypes—the assumptions and biases that cloud the judgment of those who are supposed to be helping us. It's like they're looking at us through a distorted lens, unable to see the real us beneath the surface.

"I was pushed off a 15-foot flight of stairs to the ground and beaten with a glass bottle in front of my children. I had a bad life of being beaten every day, hit with stuff and criticized" [...] "I'm safe [now], but on my own... they don't really provide options for help... then I overheard shelter staff make derogatory statements about me and why I stayed in the relationship." —Bobbi

Sis, breathe... this is a lot. However, I want you to be informed and empowered. You may be in an abusive relationship. And right now, you're second guessing whether to leave or how to leave if you're only going to face more challenges and

43

discrimination. I am not trying to deter you from seeking support from a shelter, social services, or church. Again, I want you to be informed about how racism is ingrained in our society and impacts us when seeking support. This information is empowering, but please know that revictimization is still very possible. Press forward anyway because you deserve a relationship free of violence, and everyone's experience is different.

Racism and Societal Stressors

Black women often experience racial discrimination and societal stressors that mix in with the trauma of domestic violence. Racism can intersect with domestic violence, resulting in unique forms of harm and marginalization. More barriers. I will add this: all of the participants experienced racism and discrimination when they attempted to access resources for domestic violence. Awareness of discrimination, negative stereotyping, and the vulnerability of Black men to police brutality are all factors that can discourage Black women from seeking help with domestic violence, and thus contribute to the high rates of domestic violence that they experience.

"You don't call the unsaved, so that did away with calling the police because Christians were supposed to deal in a Christian way with Christian people in their own group. To call in the unsaved was forbidden. So that blocked you from being able to get out of the relationship and seek help." —Carla

That's just how deep the fear of abuse runs in Black women. We don't even want our Black men to experience it at the expense of us. So, we stay in it. We stay for the abuse with the idea that we're the saviors because we know the historical relationship between our Black men and the police.

These cultural barriers often discourage Black women from reporting or escaping battering situations. For example, the procedures that women have to follow to get assistance, such as filing protective orders and finding shelters and career services, can be intimidating. Due to systemic oppression, Black women do not have nearly as many resources available to them as other women do. Black women lack access to necessary support such as counseling, financial services, and housing. These examples throughout this chapter and book illustrate how patterns of oppression intersect in Black women's experiences with domestic violence.

Do you need more receipts? Remember Bobbi? She overheard shelter staff make derogatory statements about her. One study points out that racist practices in community services like the police, government agencies, and shelters make things harder for women of color (Sharma, 2001). I didn't stutter, the entities that are supposed to serve and protect contribute to the struggles. Because of the long history of oppression by White society, many of us may distrust White-led agencies and services, and that keeps us from seeking help.

"I couldn't understand why they helped the Hispanic women, and told me they didn't have any help for women like me." — *Tina*

Still to this day, racism is like the elephant in the room, always there but nobody wants to address it. But the truth is, it's a big part of why so many of us find ourselves trapped in abusive relationships. From facing discrimination when we try to get help to just dealing with the constant stress of being Black in America, it's like we're fighting an uphill battle every step of the way. But you know what? We're strong, sis. We're warriors, fighting against the odds and refusing to be silenced. And as a therapist, I've learned that sometimes, it takes a combination of things to truly understand the complexities of our experiences.

Let's continue to remember this: we're not just survivors, we're sisters. And together, we'll navigate the twists and turns of this journey, lifting each other up and finding strength in our collective resilience.

Gender and Sexual Orientation

Now, let's talk about something that hits close to home for a lot of us: traditional gender roles. You know, those old-fashioned ideas about what men and women should be like and who we should be with? Well, turns out, they can cause a whole lot of trouble, especially when it comes to relationships. See, gender roles rooted in patriarchy can create this idea that men should be tough and in control, while women should be submissive and obedient. It's like a script we're all supposed to follow, whether we like it or not. And when things don't go according to plan, it can lead to some pretty harmful dynamics in relationships. Some of these same issues can occur in same-sex relationships. Oop! Same-sex relationships aren't exempt from experiencing domestic violence. Same-sex relationships can be abusive too. We can see this through Rachel.

Rachel's story of abuse started in childhood when she witnessed domestic violence between her parents. It continued when she was in foster care, group homes, and even when her mother regained custody of her. As Rachel matured, she found herself in abusive same-sex relationships.

Let's paint an even more vivid picture: you're a Black woman in a same-sex relationship, hurting, scared, and desperate for someone to understand. Your partner, who you once loved deeply, has become abusive, and you feel trapped and isolated. Your sexual orientation adds another layer of difficulty, making it harder to find help. For example, many domestic violence shelters and support services are geared towards heterosexual women, leaving you feeling unseen and unsupported. Also, due to homophobia, LGBT+ survivors are denied assistance and domestic violence services. Family and friends may not fully accept your same-sex relationship either, causing you to worry that they won't be there for you if you reveal the abuse. The fear of being outed or threatening to reveal someone's sexual orientation/gender identity is often used as a controlling tactic, creating a barrier for seeking assistance. Furthermore, discrimination from police and social services looms large, as you worry they won't take your situation seriously because you're both Black and a lesbian.

"I was a member and worked for the church as an office administrator for two years, paid my tithes, and when they found out the abuse was from a female, they pushed me away and out the door." —Rachel

Many Black LGBT+ survivors like Rachel, are not taken seriously when they speak out about the abuse they experience in their same-sex relationships. For quite some time, the domestic violence movement focused on heterosexual relationships; hence, LGBT+ relationships were left out of the movement. Some never say another word because they do not want to be judged by their sexual orientation. The fear of being dismissed, ridiculed, or further marginalized keeps them silent. They carry the heavy burden of their trauma alone, knowing that reaching out might lead to more pain instead of relief.

Imagine the courage it takes to finally confront abuse only to be met with disbelief or condemnation because of who you love. The intersection of race, gender, and sexual orientation creates a unique and often unrecognized barrier to seeking help. Black women in same-sex relationships face a double-edged sword: fighting the stigma of domestic violence and the prejudice against their sexual orientation. This double-stuffed discrimination makes seeking help even more scary.

The judgment they fear is not just from strangers but from their own communities, including the places they turn to for solace and support. The Black church, friends, family—these pillars of strength can sometimes become sources of additional pain. The lack of understanding and acceptance can push these women further into the shadows, making them feel unseen and unheard.

But here's the thing, none of us are alone because traditional gender roles and expectations can create harmful dynamics within relationships and communities. These roles and expectations reinforce power imbalances that contribute to domestic violence.

Religion/Spirituality

I believe we're spiritual beings, and our religious and spiritual beliefs shape how we see the world. These beliefs affect how we see ourselves and how we interact with others. Traditional gender roles are often rooted in patriarchy, and that shows up in many religions and spiritual practices too. For instance, some religions define women by roles like caretakers, peacekeepers, wives, and mothers, meaning they might endure abuse just to keep the family together. A lot of religions push women to forgive and to "stick it out" or "pray and stay."

Because of this, you might feel like leaving goes against God's principles of marriage and that you'd be selfish for choosing yourself over family, especially if kids are involved. Since divorce is a big "NO" in many religions, you might feel like you've failed your faith for choosing to leave an abusive relationship. Plus, religious or spiritual beliefs shape how abusers are viewed, so you might get questioned about your wifey duties, like "what did you do" or if you provoked the abuse. This can make you feel guilty and mess with your mind.

Here's the tea: religious and spiritual identity is a unique challenge for many Black women survivors. It can either help or hold you back. We'll dig deeper into this in Chapter 4.

The Beginning of The End

All of the women mentioned reported experiencing multiple oppressions due to their intersecting identities of race, gender, religion, socioeconomic status, and sexual orientation.

For far too long have the complexities of Black women's encounters with domestic violence remained buried beneath societal norms and systemic barriers. It's as if these complexities have been "loc'd up," tightly bound and concealed from view. But it's time to disrupt this pattern, to dismantle the barriers that have hindered progress and perpetuated suffering.

I know it looks like we have the short end of the stick, but amid the darkness, there is a paradoxical light of hope: spirituality. For many Black women, spirituality serves as a coping mechanism—a source of solace and strength in the face of trouble. As we delve deeper into this book, we will explore how spirituality intersects with the other dimensions of Black women's experiences with domestic violence, shedding light on pathways to healing and empowerment.

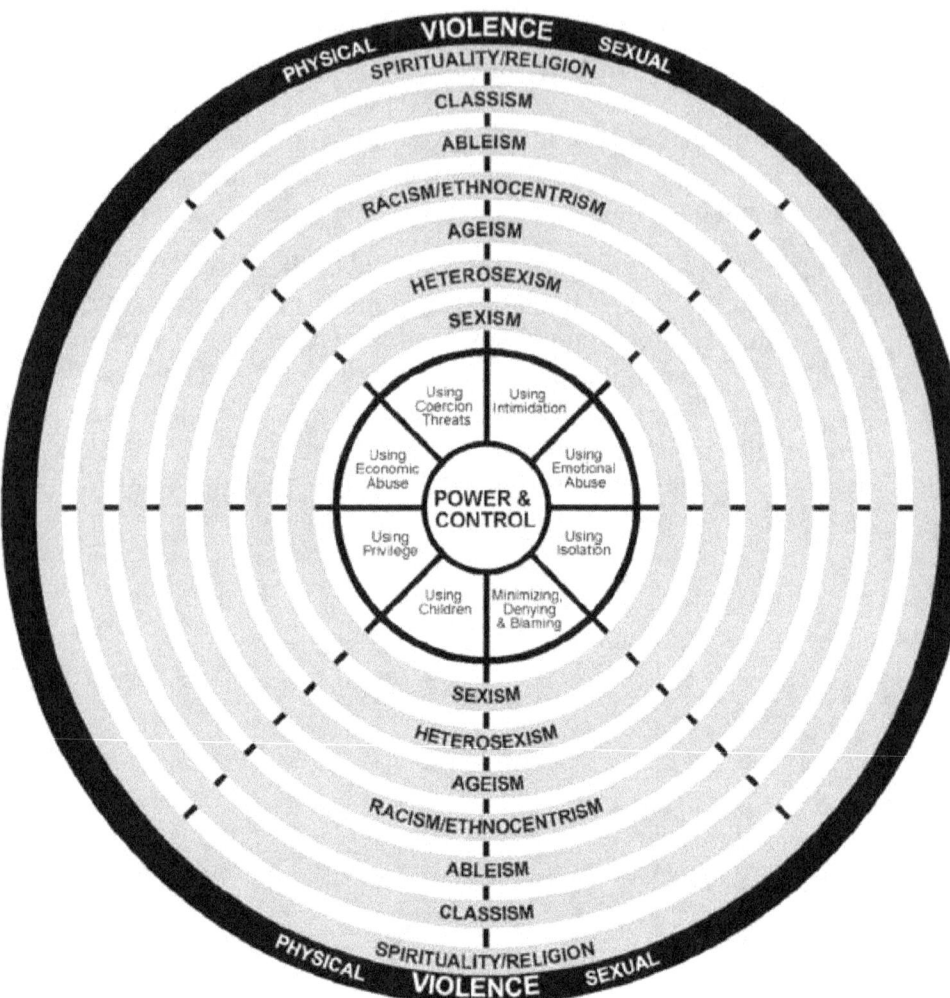

Activity 3.

Review the Multicultural Power & Control Wheel and reflect on your experiences as a Black woman with the following prompts.

1. In what ways have various systems of oppression (racism, discrimination, religion, sexism, etc.) shaped your domestic violence experience?

2. How has your identity as a Black woman affected how you

feel/felt about leaving the relationship?

3. In what ways can your intersectional identities empower you in your journey of healing from domestic violence?

4. Have you ever felt pressure to be strong, even when you were hurting? What were the consequences?

Chapter 3. Understanding Domestic Violence Trauma

"Trauma is not your final resting place." —Alex Elle

What is Trauma

By now you have learned that domestic violence is not easily understood and very complex. Abusers utilize various tactics such as manipulation, isolation, humiliation, coercion, and physical attacks to maintain power and control over you. As a result, you are constantly living in a warzone: a vicious cycle of fear and tension. This persistent threat to safety, uncertainty, and walking on eggshells is traumatic and impacts your physical, emotional, and spiritual health. With that being said, understanding trauma and the impact of domestic violence trauma is essential to your healing journey. Why, because, when you understand trauma and are aware of how it manifests for you, you are better able to advocate for yourself. **Content warning:** This chapter contains discussion of domestic violence trauma, including emotional, physical, and sexual abuse. Content may be distressing for some readers, particularly those with live experiences of violence or trauma. This chapter also helps you gain clarity on how trauma affects your brain, body, emotions, and relationships. Please prioritize your well-being while engaging with this material. Consider taking breaks, reaching out for support, or skipping sections if needed.

According to the American Psychiatric Association, a traumatic experience threatens your psychological or physical safety, causing overwhelming, intense feelings of fear, lack of control, helplessness, disempowerment and changes how you view yourself, the world or others (2000). The National Child Traumatic Stress Network defines trauma as a single event or series of events that involve fear or threat and overwhelms an individual's ability to cope. You can visit the website here:

As a therapist, I explain to clients that trauma is what happened to you, and how your body or nervous system responds to what happened. Trauma is a deep wound that sometimes you don't know is even there; it is based on past events impacting you presently. For example, frequent statements I often hear from clients during intake sessions are, "I would like help with outbursts, or expressing my feelings", "I want to understand why I shut down or why I take things so personally." Or, "I want to stop being so defensive, and be able to accept feedback." Essentially, they are describing how current behaviors connected to past trauma are impacting their relationships with people, colleagues, God, children, etc. The funny thing is that they don't connect the behavior to a traumatic event. So after explaining what trauma is, I often get asked, "Are you sure, it's trauma, I mean, I wouldn't call it that", "Why isn't it a bad experience?"

My response is if the bad experience impacted your thoughts about yourself, how you perceive others, your behavior, it is trauma. The truth is trauma is universal; nobody is exempt. Everyone at some point in their life has experienced trauma. Also, everybody experiences trauma differently; two people can grow up together and experience the same trauma, but it can mean something different for each person, but still hurts the same.

Different types of Trauma

You can experience trauma in two ways: 1) Big T—a significant event that leaves you feeling powerless and fearing for your life such as a car accident, natural disaster, or assault, and 2) Little t—events that are not life threatening or cause bodily harm, but cause distress and impact your ability to cope with the experience such as divorce or infidelity in a relationship. As mentioned above, trauma can occur as single or recurring, but also trauma can occur as complex, developmental, and

53

intergenerational trauma. I wholeheartedly believe trauma is trauma, whether it is big "T" or little "t", but clarifying how it shows up helps normalize your experience and is a form of empowerment. Below are various types of trauma:

- Single or acute event: car accident, loss or bereavement, natural disaster, witnessing something terrible happen to someone, divorce.

- Recurring: domestic violence, childhood sexual abuse, bullying, neglect.

- Complex trauma: series of events that happened over a long period of time (months or years), i.e., domestic violence, medical trauma, chronic neglect and abandonment, human trafficking, and parentification (children taking on adult roles).

- Developmental trauma: trauma that occurred during early childhood, i.e., abuse, neglect, or abandonment from parents.

- Intergenerational: trauma passed down through generations, i.e., slavery, the Holocaust, and domestic violence.

As you can see, domestic violence can be recurring, complex, and intergenerational trauma. For many Black women, that traumatic experience can span from childhood through generations. For instance, Tina witnessed her mother get physically beaten every day. "We had a lot of domestic violence in our home. I watched my mom get beat every day; not every other day... but **every** day. My grandfather also beat my grandmother." Tina is describing generations of abuse in her family. I am aware of many cousins that experienced abuse and stayed in the relationship. I also witnessed abuse. To add to that, my abusive relationship and the research participants' relationships were examples of complex trauma because there were many forms of abuse and power and control.

How your Brain & Body Responds to Trauma

As a therapist, I find that helping survivors understand their brain (central nervous system) and how trauma has impacted them is a pivotal part of the healing process. Likewise, I had to understand why I would raise my voice when I felt disrespected, and why I found myself in the same type of relationships. So, I gained some clarity about the brain and nervous system.

Our nervous system consists of two systems: the parasympathetic nervous system (PNS) and sympathetic nervous system (SNS). In an ideal world, they complement each other for survival and safety. The PNS, which I consider my favorite, relaxes the body during periods of high stress by releasing hormones to slow down stress responses as a result of fear or danger. The PNS gives the body a calming and relaxing feeling over a period of time. I was introduced to the PNS system during graduate school, when my nutritionist suggested I try yoga and mindfulness activities to balance the stress of school. I did not realize at the time how stress was impacting my body until I engaged in restful activities for relaxation.

The SNS activates the flight or fight responses during high periods of stress. The unique thing about the SNS is that the responses happen so quickly that the body is instantly prepared to defend and protect itself from fear. Usually, when you experience distress, the SNS and PNS collaborate, and your body returns to a normal state when the threat has passed. For example, running late to catch a flight, but relaxing after arriving at your gate to board the plane. However, your system works differently when it experiences trauma. When you experience a traumatic event, your brain alerts your body that you are in danger, and your body goes into protection mode to address the threat. That protection mode is either through dissociation or hyperarousal, aka "high alert."

Let me break down dissociation - when you go through a traumatic experience, your brain can get overwhelmed and go into survival mode. Sometimes, to protect yourself, you dissociate - meaning mentally "check out" or separate from what's happening. It's like your mind leaves your body for a bit to avoid feeling the full pain or fear. Also, because you aren't fully present during the trauma, your brain doesn't store the memory the way it usually would. Instead of saving it like a complete, clear story, the memory gets broken up into fragments - fragmented memory - little pieces like random images, sounds, feelings, or body sensations without a clear beginning, middle, and end. Later on, when you try to remember the event, it might feel jumbled, confusing, or like pieces are missing. You might remember flashes of it, but not the full story - and sometimes those fragments can pop up out of nowhere, like in nightmares, flashbacks, or strong emotional reactions. For example, while writing this chapter, I took several breaks because I was triggered and I had random blurry clips of the abuse.

This hyperarousal is known as the 4Fs trauma response: Fight, Flight, Freeze or Fawn, and your brain and body may respond in a variety of ways when it feels threatened. Even after the danger of the trauma has passed, our brain can still respond as if danger is present. The physiological responses can look like peaks in cortisol levels, increases in heart rates and breathing, sweaty palms, clenched fists, an increase in rate of speech or tone of voice, cloudy thoughts, and difficulty concentrating. Trauma can push our nervous system outside its ability to cope and self-regulate. For some people, your system feels "on" all the time and unable to relax. For others, your system is "off", and you are disconnected, fatigued, or depressed. Many can alternate between the highs and lows, but in the case of chronic stress and complex trauma such as domestic violence, your nervous system becomes conditioned to living in a constant state of fear.

Through the lens of abusive relationships, let's review the 4Fs:

Fight Response: When you perceive danger, you respond with aggression. You are physically fighting or verbally fighting (arguments), pulling or struggling to get away. For survivors that also experience sexual assault, you may hit, push, or "say no" to fight off the abuser. When this response manifests, beliefs are impacted, and you tend to blame yourself for the altercation; you feel you are an abuser too. Or, you may feel frustrated or upset because you were not strong enough to get away or end the abuse. However, that is far from the truth. What is true is that when your body felt threatened, the fight response automatically responded to the danger. Whether it was verbal or physical blows, you were trying to survive the threat; it was not your fault.

Flight Response: When you perceive danger, you escape from the threat by distancing yourself from the threat. For example, you feel some tension and fear when the abuser enters the room, and there is no way to survive, so you leave the room. Or, you may avoid places or activities when you feel overwhelmed or distract yourself from the situation.

Freeze Response: Also known as the camouflage response, when you perceive danger, you may get silent, still, or tense when immobilized by fear due to a threat. For instance, the abuser verbally and emotionally attacks you, and you remain silent or find you have the inability to speak, or you may also "freeze" to avoid escalating arguments. For survivors that have experienced sexual assault, you may have laid still or played "dead" to avoid further danger in hopes that the abuser will leave you alone. Or, you may not remember anything, as the body shuts down to cope with the danger. Essentially, the body is experiencing a physical or emotional paralysis; unable to move or think.

Fawn Response: When you perceive danger, for safety, you keep the peace and avoid conflict by appeasing the wishes and needs of the abuser. You may over apologize and blame yourself for everything, avoid expressing your feelings, and just be overly nice, i.e., bending over backwards to survive the threat. You act as if your needs, rights, and boundaries do not matter, and you make yourself uncomfortable to please others.

Understanding Triggers

Trauma returns as a reaction, belief, or symptom, but not feeling. That reaction is called a trigger. I teach clients that when you are triggered, a painful wound, trauma, or distressful experience is resurfaced. When we experience trauma, we do not know how it is stored in our body, often the memories are not stored in a healthy way. It is stored based on what we are feeling and sensing in the moment. Therefore, when our brain and body recognizes a similarity between our past and present, the 4Fs response system is activated; in other words, we are triggered. The uniqueness about triggers is that these responses are automatic; we do not choose them. My EMDR Consultant provided this great metaphor to remember triggers that I frequently share with clients: visualize a melting ice cube; trauma freezes the memory (ice cube), and triggers thaw it (melting ice cube).

Trauma overwhelms our body's capacity to cope, and similar negative experiences fires it back up. Triggers stimulate the function of the experience; of what happened to you. It ignites past wounds as if we are experiencing them in the present. Also, triggers are unique to each person, are complex, and manifest in a variety of ways. They can be any sensory reminder of an event such as sight, sound, smell, touch, and taste. In addition, they can be a specific time of day, season, song, and image. To add to that, unanswered texts, calls, or emails can trigger feelings of abandonment for adults that experience neglect or childhood abandonment. Lastly, triggers can look like anger, crying, yelling, being alone, defensive, rejection, fear of judgment, violence in the news, breakups, or unwanted touching. Keep in mind that triggers will happen as long as you are alive because our nervous system is still working. The key is that you get to a place in which triggers don't overwhelm or flood you.

By now, I hope you are connecting your experiences and triggers and have more clarity on why you do what you do. If you are triggered, activate your PNS and take a few deep breaths and remind yourself that you are safe. I've worked with clients that have been out of the abusive relationship for over 20 years and still trying to manage triggers—essentially connecting the dots on how the trauma has impacted their body. I never made the connection between my mind, body, and behavior until a few years ago. When I am triggered, my heart races, my speech increases, and I tend to raise my voice. Literally, preparing for battle. Sometimes, I may not remember what I do or say when I am triggered, also known as fragmented memory. In other words, due to high emotions and dissociation from the trauma, memories are spotty. For example, I had an experience in which I felt disrespected by a guy. The experience activated a past experience in which I was extremely disrespected.

Here's the memory that was triggered: on the day my father was funeralized, my abuser told me he was engaged. Yep, he was seeing two people at the same time. The level of HURT was inexpressible. I felt tremendously disrespected and dismissed by this malicious act. So, whenever I felt disrespected, I was triggered. Going back to the example where I was disrespected by a guy – he stated I sounded all over the place and went off on him. Honestly, I don't remember what all I said. Months later, I found myself triggered again when I tried to communicate my feelings. He shared that I was rambling, and I was because 1) I had not experienced a safe space to be vulnerable, and 2) I did not realize that ever existed. I was used to conflict and was prepared for battle.

I am grateful for this illuminating experience, as it propelled me forward to dig a little deeper about how my past domestic violence trauma was still present for me. However, when I was triggered the second time while trying to express my feelings, I found some hope and optimism. I was able to reflect on the difference in the triggers and pull on my strength to confront those triggers. It was at this moment that I heard an inner voice say "come heal this part of me." My faith reminded me that not every trigger is meant to destroy me; I had to address it for healing. This trigger was an alert that the key to freedom was facing past wounds. For me, it was a form of empowerment and self-love to confront triggers and provide language to what happened to me.

Break and Breathe

We have covered a lot so far in this chapter. You may find yourself reflecting on previous and current events and are triggered. Your body and thoughts return to that moment, and you begin to feel that you are not safe. Consider, is it more so a warning, or are you currently in danger? Now pause and take a deep breath, center your experiences, and notice how your body responds. Close your eyes, do a body scan, and notice what you are feeling. If you notice any distress, acknowledge it and go back to your breath. The breath is the connection between your mind and body; slowly breathe.

Grounding techniques are helpful in distracting you from a myriad of emotions, sensations, and thoughts. Grounding exercises incorporate senses and visualization to help you reconnect to the present moment. The exercises "ground" you in the present moment for safety and a state of calmness. I find this self-regulation technique very helpful and frequently used during sessions.

5, 4, 3, 2, 1 Technique

Utilizing your senses and paying attention to your surroundings, think of 5 things you can see, 4 things you can feel, 3 things you can hear, 2 things you can smell, and 1 thing you can taste.

Reflection Prompts

When you are ready, ask yourself the following questions:

1. How am I triggered?

2. What was this grounding exercise like?

3. In what ways do I manage triggers, and what can I now do differently?

4. In what way have I disconnected from myself?

How Domestic Violence Trauma Look: Effects of Domestic Violence Trauma

In many instances, domestic violence is invisible in that we cannot see it like we see physical wounds. It can manifest in a variety of ways such as Post Traumatic Stress Disorder (PTSD), anxiety, depression, insomnia, stomach problems, nightmares, withdrawal, autoimmune diseases, and unexplained aches and pain. Research has found that the lingering effects of abuse can have lasting and, for some, debilitating effects. For example, survivors struggle with frequent headaches, grief, insomnia, and eating disorders, and some live with chronic ailments and post traumatic symptoms for the rest of their lives. Also, as a result of the detrimental effects of domestic violence, you are left with feelings of guilt, shame, low self-esteem, powerlessness, and helplessness, and frequently question your decisions.

I want to expand on PTSD because it is a very common diagnosis for survivors of abuse. When people think of PTSD, they automatically think of veterans that have served in a war. Abuse is far from their mind, but an abusive relationship is just that—an emotional and physical war zone. You are always guarded, prepared for battle. Sami shared: *"the relationship was scary and walking on eggshells. I never knew what was going to set him off. He was insecure and consistently accused me of flirting with people; I was always guarded."*

PTSD can look different for everyone; for some, it's difficulty expressing the details of events, re-experiencing memories of the event, avoidant behavior, being easily startled, nightmares, self-blame, angry outbursts, and emotional activation. For others, the symptoms can diminish and resurface at a later time, or you turn to various substances to manage the symptoms. Rachel shared: *"It is a struggle every day to wake up being scared of somebody, not knowing what mood he was in. I've been hospitalized more than once... I had my teeth knocked out... little stuff like that. I've been kidnapped and thrown in a car trunk... raped... even had to medicate myself the street pharmacist way to drown out what was going on."*

Research tells us that trauma impacts our body, brain development, brain chemistry, behavior, and beliefs. While abuse takes a toll on your entire body, the psychological damage to your belief system is underestimated. Many survivors that experience abuse have a hard time identifying with it because they are not physically wounded. However, the repeated shame, gaslighting, name-calling, and belittling can leave you feeling powerless and hopeless. At times it can be so subtle that you do not think you are experiencing abuse. The tactics of emotional abuse are meant to erase your sense of worth and confidence; the main goal is disempowerment and disconnection from others. For example, isolation from family and friends, monitoring your whereabouts and social media, dismissive behavior, accusations, flipping the switch or blaming you for something, humiliation, and guilt. Over time, these repeated abusive patterns take a toll on your emotions, thoughts, and begin to wear you down. As a result, you isolate yourself from others and believe you are not worthy, you deserve the abuse, it is your fault, you are not good enough.

When my abuser disrespected me on the day of my father's funeral, a bunch of negative core beliefs about myself surfaced. I like to refer to these beliefs as "Negative Nancy." Negative Nancy aka "inner critic" repeatedly whispered: "I am not good enough," "I am not important," "I cannot choose good partners", "I don't matter." These beliefs really dampened my self-worth and spirit. Negative Nancy was loud, bold...a big BULLY! To help you reframe negative core beliefs like "I am not worthy", I invite you to try this exercise grounded in Cognitive Behavioral Therapy (CBT). CBT is a type of therapy that helps you understand how your thoughts, feelings, and actions are connected. CBT techniques are critical for reframing negative core thoughts after experiencing abuse, as they empower you to challenge self-blame, replace unhelpful beliefs with healthier perspectives, and rebuild a sense of self-worth and control over your lives.

Reframing the Story You've Been Told:

1. Write down a belief about yourself that continues to cause pain or self-doubt.

2. Trace Where it Came From – Ask Yourself: Where did this belief come from? Who first made me feel this way?

3. Gently Question It: Is this belief always true? Would I say this to someone I love?

4. Speak a new truth: Create a statement that affirms your worth and healing. "I am worthy of love and healing", "I matter and deserve peace."

5. Reclaim Your Voice: "Even though I use to believe_____, I now choose to believe_____ because_____.

Disconnection

From my experiences as a survivor, counselor, and researcher, I have learned that trauma can lead to disconnection from oneself. In an abusive relationship, you detach from yourself to survive and engage in survival techniques to sustain the relationship. Just think, how could you endure such blatant disrespect and harm without finding a way to survive? Survival techniques are ways you protect yourself in a situation you never should have had to face. When you're in an abusive situation: 1) your body and mind did what they needed to do to survive; 2) you do not realize you are disconnected from yourself because you're trying to survive. Ask yourself, did you stay quiet, tried to keep the peace, or told yourself it wasn't that bad just to get through the day? Yeah, I have too; you are not alone. Survival techniques can range from the following:

- Over-explaining.

- Justifying everything you do.
- Doing things ahead to ensure things are going smoothly (attempts to stay in the honeymoon stage) such as ironing clothes, fixing breakfast or lunch, rationalizing groceries or money to avoid arguments.
- Shutting down emotionally to keep from feeling overwhelmed.
- Stayed because you had no safe way to leave.
- Told yourself it was love because it started that way.
- Fighting back.

Some frequent survival techniques I used were over-explaining, keeping the peace, jumping through hoops, rationalizing why I spent money on things to avoid arguments over finances, emotional eating, and suppressing my feelings. Now, survival techniques can be a hard concept to accept, because you've repeatedly been told the abuse is your fault. However, the more you learn about domestic violence, you will begin to accept that abuse is about power and control - and no one ever deserves to be mistreated, hurt, or manipulated. But, if you're still struggling with releasing the belief that the "abuse IS your fault", I want you to think of ways you resisted the violence, even in small moments. Create a "Survival Map", marking moments where you made choices that protected yourself emotionally, mentally, or physically. The goal is to shift the narrative from victimhood to resilience, showing your agency and strength to survive. You will see that you were not weak, but you were strong and resourceful. You did what you had to do in order to stay safe, protect your children, or survive another day. That takes strength, even if it doesn't always feel that way.

Another reason you do not realize you are disconnected and in survival mode is due to the following three reasons:

1. Love—you love your partner and really want the relationship to work.

2. Trauma bonding—when you form a deep emotional

attachment to a person who is abusive or harmful. It often occurs because of a cycle of abuse mixed with kindness or affection, which creates confusion and makes it hard to leave the relationship. It's like being stuck in a toxic connection where the good moments make you overlook or tolerate the bad ones; and

3. Hope—you're holding on to hope, this fantasy, and unable to see reality.

Now, don't get me wrong; there is nothing wrong with being hopeful because hope contributes to a positive attitude and well-being. For me, my hope was rooted in "if I just get it right" or "if I did it this way," the abuse would stop. However, that hope became a distortion of reality. I didn't realize the cycle of abuse and power dynamics were destabilizing me. I found myself holding onto hope as I recalled many happy moments in the relationship and somehow thought we could get back there. Then repeated moments of "I am sorry", "you should've listened to me", "you are beautiful", "I will make it up to you," reeled me back into the cycle. Just a bunch of victim-blaming.

When asked about disconnection, Sami shared: *"At times, I thought there was hope for the relationship, but after this most recent experience, I realized my life was spared, and I could not go back to the cycle of abuse I had endured for over 10 years."*

Rachel shared: *"I even had to medicate myself the street pharmacist way to drown out what was going on.*

For Tina, she described her family as very spiritual and religious, but also dysfunctional and hypocritical. For example, her grandfather was a minister and had physically abused her grandmother, his daughter, and grandchildren. In addition, her grandmother stayed active in the church and told the family to follow the commandments in the Bible, yet their family is full of many abusers and heavy alcohol drinkers. As a result of this violent and chaotic environment, Tina's cognitive dissonance between her desire to follow her family's religious teachings and the stressors in her life was a reason that she became angry at the confusion and kept a shell around herself to detach from the distress.

As you can see, you can walk on eggshells and stay in this constant vicious cycle of abuse, not realizing your hope and disconnection is misguided to stay in the abuse versus a vision towards a life free from violence. Ignoring my feelings led to so much confusion that I lost sight of some fundamentals such as the right to express my feelings, say no, respect, and safety. Instead, this disconnection manifested as anxiety, insomnia, low self worth, lack of confidence, insecurity, weight gain, and fear of loneliness. I realized many of you may be on the fence, or you want to stay as a form of empowerment, thinking you can change their behavior, but the more you dishonor yourself, the more you lose the essence of who you are. As you begin or continue healing, I want you to carry this with you: You are not to blame; I did things to protect myself; I am not broken.

Guilt & Shame

My self-worth was at its lowest after the relationship ended. On one hand, the relationship was over, but the impact of the abuse on my psychological wellbeing was lingering. I found myself out of the relationship and emotionally trapped. Essentially, I was in mental bondage. I felt so guilty and ashamed for what I endured because I was manipulated to believe the abuse was my fault. It was my fault for the way my abuser acted—he repeatedly told me I brought it on myself. It was my fault for leaving and going back multiple times. It was my fault for protecting him when my grandmother told me she didn't like how he talked to me. It was my fault for EVERYTHING. For instance, I grew up hearing it takes two to tangle, and I felt I was somehow responsible for the abuse. So much so that I wanted to protect him due to what other people may think of him and of me. The weight of other people's perceptions weighed on me heavily. The feelings of guilt and shame lingered for many years that I suffered in silence and didn't tell close family and friends. Even while writing this book, I was in a tug of war over whether I should share this, or what people think of me, my mother, and sisters. However, the more I wrote, the more liberated I felt and affirmed myself with these affirmations:

- I have a right to share my story; my story is unique to me.

- My voice is powerful, and sharing my truth is an act of courage and healing.

- I am worthy of being heard and supported.

- I release fear and embrace my strength.

- My story has the power to inspire, heal, and create change—for myself and others.

What I have realized from my personal, clinical, and research experience is that overcoming guilt and shame is a profound journey for Black women survivors. It is a journey shaped by the unique cultural, social, and historical burdens we often carry. Many of us feel an added weight of strength, resilience, and independence—a stereotype that can make seeking help feel like a betrayal of their community's expectations. This sense of duty can intensify feelings of guilt and self-blame, as we may question if we somehow "failed" by experiencing abuse. Reframing these beliefs is crucial, as we must recognize that abuse is never your fault and that vulnerability does not equate to weakness. Also, with compassion and support, you can start to view your decision to prioritize your safety and mental health as a profound act of courage and self-respect.

Now shame is on another level, as I feel it is more deeply rooted than guilt. It makes you think something is wrong with you. For example, I felt guilty for experiencing abuse, and internalized that I am a bad person or I am not worthy of healthy relationships, so it's better to stay in an abusive relationship. Afterall, it's my fault. But the longer you stay silent, the deeper shame permeates your belief system, resulting in feelings of depression, lower confidence, self-esteem, and makes you question who you are.

Shame can also manifest in interpersonal relationships. Let's revisit Negative Nancy; she kept badgering me, over and over again like a nagging mosquito that would not go away. Invisible wounds that would persistently show up. For example, if I didn't get a job that I felt I was qualified for, I thought I wasn't good enough, that I wasn't smart enough, or I lacked something. Every relationship that didn't work out, I felt it was my fault, that I am not good enough; I am a bad person. Essentially, rejection triggered these negative thoughts and deepened shame. Whenever I would experience an event that triggered the belief "I am not good enough," the belief was validated; it was reinforced. This cycle lasted for many years, and it wasn't until the pandemic that I began to take a closer look at myself and asked why am I like this? So, I began working with a trauma therapist to understand my thoughts and behavior, which helped me see how the trauma from domestic violence was stored in both my body and brain. This insight became a turning point, allowing me to release guilt and shame and to fully embrace the truth that the abuse was **NEVER** my fault and that abusers are solely responsible for their actions.

Reflection Prompts

- Guilt implies that you did something wrong, such as causing harm to another person. Think of your "guilt" and ask yourself, "What harm did I cause the abuser? Why do I believe I hold responsibility for this situation?

- What would my life feel like without this guilt?

- What can I do today to begin releasing it?

- If your experience with trauma had a voice, what would you say about how it has tried to shape your identity?

CHAPTER 4: WE'VE COME THIS FAR BY FAITH

FYI: I am not a minister or theologian, but I encourage you to read this chapter. It's givin' self-awareness and enlightenment. Read this chapter if you want to gain awareness about the significance of faith, spirituality, and religion for Black women and how it can impact your decision to stay or leave. I know what you're thinking, but "this ain't that." This is not an attempt to force religious beliefs. Yes, the biblical texts in this chapter are provided from a Christian perspective, but guess what? Domestic violence crosses ALL religious denominations.

What's that one Black hymn you can't seem to forget? You know the one that's on page 200 and something, but you've heard it so many times you know it by heart and don't even have to look for the page. For me it's: "We've come this far by Faith" by Rev. Milton Biggham. This song is like the hymn of all hymns. It provides hope and encouragement for the future, and a reminder that with confidence in the Lord's help, you will get through whatever you are facing now or in the future. Without question, it provides assurance, comfort, and peace. Go read the lyrics for yourself, and you'll see. I asked that initial question to show the impact of the intersection of faith, spirituality, and religion for the Black community. For me, this hymn strengthens my faith, draws me closer to God, and encourages me to engage in additional spiritual practices such as prayer, meditation, and reading my Bible. Even if you couldn't think of a hymn, you more than likely thought of some kind of gospel song. Grab that song in your mind as you read this chapter. This chapter honors the role of faith and spirituality in our lives. It explores how faith can be both a source of strength, and sometimes, a barrier to seeking help. It encourages you to reconnect with your faith in ways that support your healing.

The terms faith, spirituality, and religion are often used interchangeably, though each has its own unique and distinct definition. For the purpose of this chapter, the terms will be used interchangeably, but I want to explain the difference among them. Faith is a belief and trust in something or someone, often without needing proof. For example, having faith in a friend's honesty or in a higher power. Keep in mind, faith can mean something different to each of you. For instance, some women may define themselves as a "woman of faith" versus a "Christian woman." Spirituality is a personal sense of connection to something greater than yourself, which can involve a search for meaning in life. It doesn't have to be tied to a specific religion and include practices like mediation or nature appreciation. Religion is an organized system of beliefs or set of beliefs that typically utilizes rules and rituals related to worship and moral guidance. For instance, Christianity, Islam, and Buddhism are all religions. Pulling this together, think of faith as "knowing," spirituality as "being," and religion as "doing." For me, my faith in God strengthens my spirituality or relationship with Christ, and I attend Christian religious worship services to maintain spiritual wellness and a close connection to God.

As mentioned in Chapter 1, research indicates intersections of faith, spirituality, and religion as possible explanations for high rates of domestic violence among Black women. It plays a central role in the lives of many Black women. For instance, religion shapes a survivor's understanding and response to domestic violence. Which is why it is not surprising that many Black women turn to the Black church or pastor for assistance before seeking a trained advocate or counselor. As a Black Christian woman survivor and therapist, I understand that recognizing the role of faith, religion, and spirituality is key to a culturally competent approach with Black women survivors of domestic violence. I intentionally wrote this chapter for every Black woman that is religious, spiritual, or full of faith. You may be spiritual and not religious or spiritual and full of faith. No matter how you identify, I see you.

Now, we can't discuss faith, spirituality, and religion without mentioning the Black church. In this chapter, 'Black church' refers to any congregation and leadership - pastor and ministerial staff - where the majority of members are Black. Once you understand the role of the Black church, you'll start to see how essential the Black church is to understanding domestic violence in the Black community. Even with times changing and families moving away from religion, the Black church still has many of us in a historical chokehold. You'll see that survivors in my research study sought assistance from the Black church because the Black church has always been a source of strength and hope for the Black community before members from the congregation started causing the church hurt.

Time for a quick history lesson. Back in the day, the Black church became the heart and soul of the slave community, giving them the fellowship they couldn't find anywhere else on the plantations. Through the church, a lot of slaves learned to read and understand the Bible (Wilmore, 2006). Bible scriptures brought them some emotional relief and hope for a better future, even with all the harsh conditions they were living through. As they kept reading and learning, they became aware of the injustice of slavery (Collins & Moore, 2006). The idea of the slaves being able to read had the slave masters shook! You know what they say about finding things inside of a book. They didn't want slaves to find strength and start pushing for freedom. And that's exactly what happened. The church became the center of their fight for change. Our change.

Even after slavery was abolished, the Black church kept supporting the Black community, helping people who were supposedly free but still stuck in segregation and facing racial intimidation (Collins & Moore, 2006). In some parts of the South, Blacks and Whites sometimes went to church together, but because of racist practices, Black people often couldn't fully participate in services and other activities dominated by Whites (Collins & Moore, 2006). Despite living under white dominance, the church still met the community's spiritual, emotional, psychological, physical, and moral needs.

The feeling of discrimination and racism is what pushed Black people to create their own spaces for worship in the first place, which eventually turned into what we now know as the Black church (Lincoln, 1973). In its early days, the church provided a place for emotional relief and an escape from the brutality of plantation life (Wilmore, 2006). Today, the Black church remains a powerful institution. It's still the center of Black political activity.

As you can see, research shows that the Black church has always been a rock for our community. To be honest, understanding the Black church is also key to understanding the lives of many Black people, even yourself (Worthan, 2009). Did you know over half of Black Americans go to church at least once a week (Pew Research Center, 2009)? I am not just talking about the old churches with the squeaky floors and pews. I am talking about "allofum." *Black church* is actually a term used to talk about the overall institution of Black American Christians. I know these days we go to church from the living room, but not too long ago, the Black church was the go-to place for socializing, meetings, religious, spiritual, and community needs (Plunkett, 2014).

Like I said before, we still see some Black churches heavily involved with providing clothes and shelter, financial help, and education (Zuckerman et al., 2003). Black churches still run programs that help the poor, boost community development, support families, promote health education, encourage civil rights, and support at-risk youth (Ellison et al., 2012). You may not see these efforts yourself, especially if you are not plugged into that network, or you may just see it being done by the mega churches. Whether it's through giving out clothes, money, or just a place to feel safe and heard, the Black church has always had our community's back. It's more than just a place to worship; it's a lifeline for many Black women and men alike.

I am almost done with my history lesson. See, this history is our history too. Sometimes we have to go back before we can move forward. Black women and men often still turn to the Black church for help with mental health issues like depression, anxiety, and grief, and believe it or not, relationship problems. The Black church is seen, for most, as a safe haven, a place where you can find guidance and make sense of your experiences. The Black church is the heart of the Black community regardless of if you have disconnected from it. Today, the Black church continues to be a place where you can express and practice all forms of art like dance, songs, music, preaching, and teaching every week. For these reasons, it makes sense why many Black women turn to the Black church for support and guidance when dealing with domestic violence. All of my research participants went to the Black church for domestic violence assistance before going to counselors, family, and friends. And, their first point of contact at the church was a faith leader. This critical interaction highlights the pivotal role that faith leaders play in shaping the responses and support available to survivors within the church community.

Role of pastors

The church is a powerful institution in which many believers value the voice of faith leaders. Historically, our growth as a people is thanks to the leaders in the Black church. Pastors, who are like the shepherds of the church, have a unique role in dealing with the issue of domestic violence and helping Black women dealing with that abuse (Kroeger & Nason-Clark, 2010; Miles, 2002). Thus, it is crucial for pastors to understand their role in domestic violence and the influence they have on Black women's decisions about leaving abusive relationships. However, a survey by Lifeway Research showed that 42% of Protestant pastors rarely or never talk about domestic violence in their sermons (2014), which basically sends a message that violence is okay. "The math ain't mathing."

Unfortunately, the ideal support system often falls short due to lack of domestic violence training of pastors and leaders in the church and their silence on domestic violence. Weaver et al. (2000), found that clergy are often the first people survivors turn to for help. Their survey of 1,000 battered women showed that one in three got assistance from pastors. However, this and similar studies showed that many spiritual leaders are unprepared and not very effective in dealing with domestic violence (Weaver et al., 2001; Miles, 2000). Instead of offering support and guidance, many may turn a blind eye to the suffering of their congregants, leaving them to fend for themselves in the face of violence. Or they've often responded to domestic violence with silence or denial. Even worse, some church leaders may actively encourage women to stay in abusive relationships, using twisted interpretations of biblical scriptures to justify abusive actions. For instance, Black pastors have often told women to "work harder at being a better wife," pray for strength, or submit to their husbands, promising that God wouldn't give them more than they could handle (Kroeger & Nason-Clark, 2010; Miles, 2003). The pulpit has been used to intimidate and harass survivors and enable abusers. To add to this, women have been taught to be submissive and see the man as the "head of the household." So, it's no wonder a lot of Black women turn to their (usually male) pastors for advice and feel loyal to their teachings and interpretations of the Bible when they do take the time to address it. However, because pastors lack training in spousal and partner abuse, they often don't recognize the ways abusers use emotional, physical, psychological, and sexual tactics to control their partners. Sadly, a lot of Black pastors and church leaders simply don't hold male abusers accountable.

I say all of that to say if you decide to seek counsel from a pastor or faith leader (i.e., elder, minister, etc.), I provide a few questions for consideration:

1. Trust & Safety

- Do I feel safe and comfortable discussing my experiences with this pastor?

- Do I trust this pastor to keep my conversations confidential?

74

2. Understanding & Empathy

- Have I heard sexist or victim-blaming statements from the pastor? (Women should submit and listen more to avoid abuse).

- Does this pastor have a history of showing understanding and empathy towards Black women survivors of similar experiences?

3. Training & Expertise

- What training does the pastor have in domestic violence or counseling survivors of trauma?

- Is the pastor aware or and sensitive to the specific challenges faced by Black women survivors?

1. Faith & Beliefs

- Do the pastor's beliefs and teaching align with my own faith and spiritual needs?

- How does the pastor view the role of faith and therapy in healing and recovery from trauma?

2. Past Experiences

- Have I had previous experiences with pastoral counseling, and what were the outcomes?

- How do I feel about those past experiences, and what do I want to be different this time?

3. Personal readiness

- Am I ready to discuss my experiences and begin the healing process with spiritual guidance?

- What are my goals for seeking counsel from this pastor, and how will I measure progress?

Reflecting on these questions and the answers can help in making an informed decision on seeking guidance from a faith leader. I am not saying don't do it... but if you do... don't have many expectations.

Spiritual Abuse

As noted, many Black women seek counsel from pastors and support from the church for domestic violence. However, such guidance and support can sometimes be detrimental, causing further harm. Similarly, your spiritual beliefs and religion may exacerbate feelings of disconnection, depression, and more. For instance, you may have been encouraged to "pray and stay," or be questioned about your actions, somehow implying that you are the reason for the abuse. Or, you may have been encouraged to "forgive and forget" or be more understanding and loving to end the abuse. Such guidance can cause you to question your faith and relationship with God. Additionally, you may be experiencing spiritual abuse.

No, you're not crazy. Spiritual abuse is a thing. It is a form of power and control when abusers use your faith and religious beliefs to keep you trapped in an abusive situation. This kind of abuse can really be dangerous because it twists something that is meant to be your source of strength and comfort into a weapon used against you. For example, abusers may use religious texts or doctrines to justify their actions or to convince you that leaving the relationship is "against God's will." Sadly, pastors and faith leaders also perpetuate spiritual abuse. I know this idea is disturbing, but sometimes God's people do God's work in harmful and destructive ways. This may look like telling you that suffering is a test of your faith or that you are obligated to stay and "fit" the relationships because it's your duty as a wife or partner. Quite frankly, any ministerial behavior that damages someone's relationship with God is a spiritual abuse.

Spiritual abuse can also isolate you from your church community. Some abusers will manipulate your perception of your faith community, and convince you that they won't believe you, won't support you, or that you'll be judged and ostracized if you speak out. Keep in mind that isolation is a form of power and control with a goal of keeping you away from family, friends, and resources. See, abusers want to block you from getting resources to leave, and they will take any measure to keep you disconnected and isolated. Also, that isolation can also look like refraining you from watching worship services online. This can lead to feelings of abandonment and further trap you in the cycle of abuse and fear. But "there is no fear in love. Love drives out fear." 1 John 4:18.

It's important to recognize that true faith and spirituality will never condone or tolerate abuse. Your faith should be a source of strength, not a tool for control. You should be uplifted, affirmed, and supported. If you're experiencing spiritual abuse or have experienced it, it's important to seek out supportive and understanding individuals within your faith community who can provide the correct interpretation of religious teachings— one that supports your right to a life free from abuse. Spiritual abuse occurs in all religions, and there are also interfaith and faith-based organizations specifically geared toward helping survivors of domestic violence, ensuring you receive support that aligns with your spiritual beliefs.

Remember, faith is meant to be a sanctuary, not a prison. Your spirituality should empower you, provide solace, and guide you towards a path of safety and healing. True believers emphasize that love, respect, and mutual support are central to a healthy relationship. Scriptures such as Ephesians 5:25, "Husbands, love your wives, just as Christ loved the church and gave himself up for her," highlight the importance of love and respect in relationships, not domination and control. The next section will dive into how spirituality and religion can hold Black women survivors back because of those childhood church teachings and the persuasion of church leaders.

Spirituality as an Obstacle

Spirituality, faith, and religion can serve as obstacles for Black women survivors. These obstacles come in different forms such as childhood influences and persuasion from church leaders to stay in abusive relationships. Most of the survivors I've mentioned discussed how their experiences, along with their relationships with the Black church, created a set of negative beliefs about the church that influenced whether they were going to ask for church assistance with domestic violence. Sis, brace yourself for this section—it is not all peaches and cream. It affirms what you may have experienced, are currently experiencing, and is a reminder that you are not alone.

When I asked Bobbi to describe her association with the Black church, I couldn't blame her for not wanting to speak up. I understood her to the fullest.

"I don't have a relationship with them because everyone in Black churches likes to talk about everybody's business, and I don't like that. Like, I went to them once for help for another situation, and someone told another member, and people started asking me questions . . . so it wasn't an option for me to go back to them for help." —Bobbi

Rachel's encounter gave her the same feelings; the situation was a little different. Remember, Rachel is a survivor who was in a same-sex relationship. You can already imagine the fear of even asking.

"After they pushed me out the door when they found out that I was with a female . . . they told me not to go back to them for help with anything. Then, people looked down on me and made negative comments about my children. 'They're going to end up like you. . . . it's not a good role model for them that you're in a relationship with a female.'" —Rachel

Tina, on the other hand, appreciated her experiences with the Black church but also found them puzzling.

"I've been a part of Black churches for all my life, and even as a child, I was confused about my grandmother and why she would stay with my abusive grandfather for so long, and he was a minister. I would see a lot, but I was confused about why these things were happening, but then I thought in some part of my mind I wanted to say it was normal because I saw it so much

and kept going to the Church and reading the Bible." —Tina

Both April and Carla are preacher's kids, and the images of watching their parents as ministers, along with being raised in the church, convinced them to seek the church, but April's choice ended in disappointment.

"I was raised in a predominantly Black church; there's a Bishop and his wife, people who've been in my life all my life . . . [but] they didn't help. I felt more condemned, like they forgot where they came from, and it was more of them focusing on themselves than my family needing help." —Tina

Like Tina, Carla was not surprised by the lack of care because her early experiences with the church involved seeing church members shun people for things they didn't agree with. Their experiences shaped her beliefs on how the church would respond to her domestic violence situation.

"I didn't turn to the church very much going through domestic violence, because I knew." —Carla

Sami's experience almost put the icing on the cake for me.

"My boyfriend slapped me in the church parking lot because I spoke to someone and he accused me of flirting. I asked a female minister for help to calm him down and help him understand that I was being nice and felt good after hearing the sermon. Instead, she said her husband wouldn't like her talking to anyone else." —Sami

Religious Influence in Childhood

More than half of the survivors said that being raised with certain religious beliefs made it harder for them to leave abusive relationships. Carla explained to me how her upbringing influenced her views on women and marriage.

"Spirituality was a barrier 'cause growing up, we had a lot of traditions... a lot of things we were taught that just weren't true. We grew up with the 'once married, always married to the same one' philosophy. Women can't wear pants; pants are gonna send you to hell... it was a barrier 'cause it put restrictions on

us... on what you could believe and how you could think."
—Carla

Carla was also influenced by her mother, who was a minister.

"I was raised in the church, my momma got saved when I was seven, so from seven and up I was raised in the church and had a heart for God. Since my mom is a minister, I was a preacher's kid too and was very familiar with spirituality, Christianity, and pretty much a church girl all my life... so I made many decisions and did a lot of things because my mom is a minister." —Carla

This same influence led to Carla's marriage.

"Like when I got married. Under normal circumstances, I would never have married the man, honestly; but as a good Christian girl, I didn't want to be out there fornicating and God being mad with me. So my thought process was, I've got to get married, please my mom, and make this right before God. So literally the first person that came along and said 'will you marry me,' I said yes because I wanted to have it right according to the way I was raised, then I was taught to deal with domestic violence the "Christian" way... calling in the unsaved for help was forbidden." —Carla

April, similar to Carla, was a preacher's kid, but both of her parents are pastors.

"I was raised in the church, both parents are pastors, and very protective of me. I met my ex-husband at church, and he was the only person I ever dated... I was taught to save yourself until you get married... so I married him without really knowing him and to please my parents and God. I stayed in the marriage longer than I probably should've... and tried to work on it several years so that my parents could see I was living up to the religious beliefs and things they told me." —April

Vanessa admitted that growing up, she was repeatedly instructed to take everything to God and trust he would solve it.

"I always heard to pray; believe that God is going to work it

out... and I did that and endured abuse for many years because I was taught to pray and believe God." —Vanessa

Tina reflected on her childhood and how being raised by her grandmother, also a minister's wife, impacted her. Tina shared that she hadn't left when the abuse started because her grandmother had taught her that the Bible says, "Once married, you stay with your husband."

"My grandmother stayed in the church, and [she] kept us in the word and reading the Bible. I used to love to read the red words in the Bible, as my grandmother instilled that the Bible is the ultimate source." —Tina

Church Leaders' Persuasion to Stay in the Relationship

"They say God hates divorce, and they also use that scripture as far as women submit to their husbands to encourage women to stay in the relationship." —April

Most of the women also talked about how church leaders used Bible verses to convince them to stay in their abusive relationships; this made things even harder for them. When I asked each woman how pastors or church leaders encouraged them to stay, they each had intersecting situations.

"They push you to stay 'cause they think God's gonna fix it. A pastor told me, 'Don't give up on him, don't burn that bridge, God can do this.' I felt like if I left my marriage, it was like leaving God himself. Like I was losing my faith... 'cause everything was all mixed up—what I believed, the abuse, everything." —Carla

Sami felt like pastors and leaders used scriptures like "Wives submit to your husbands" and "God hates divorce" to make women stay.

"One pastor said a man's supposed to love his wife like God loves us and to love his wife as himself, but a lot of it sounded real chauvinistic 'cause they believe the man is the head of the house and tells the wife what to do. The pastors give all authority to the man by quoting the scriptures... where the man

81

feels like he can correct you and shape you into what he thinks you should be. They're giving him the green light to do these things." —Sami

Tina and Bobbi added to the topic.

"Pastors always wanna talk about working things out or what the Bible says, but not about divorce. I was told a man's supposed to love a woman as he loves God, and then the woman's supposed to submit to the man, and it seems like from my experience that they stop there. From my past experience, what stands out is hearing pastors saying to just focus on the Lord and you do what God has called you to do and your husband will come around. I always heard the scripture about what God put together, let no man put asunder." —Tina

"They never said anything about what you may need to just kind of move on and get out of this before you really get hurt or dead; it's always just focus on the Lord. I've heard them say it's better to pray about the situation. Don't give up and just try to work it out." —Bobbi

April stated, *"They say God hates divorce, and they also use that scripture about women submitting to their husbands to make us stay."*

Similarly, Vanessa reported, *"I have heard a few men and women pastors say that Moses wrote the law on marriage and to stay in the marriage. I've heard a lot of male pastors say to stay, and I feel like the reason they said this is that some of them are abusive themselves."*

Sarah, who isn't married, heard the same scriptures but gave a different perspective on the pressure to stay. She felt pastors, leaders, and the Black church misunderstood marriage, leading to misinterpretation of scriptures.

"I think there's a stigma that every marriage is God's doing, and leaders take a lot of things in the Bible out of context, like 'you should not be divorced from your spouse.' I've heard them say, 'what God joined together let no man separate,' but if God didn't join you together in the first place, it's gonna fail, 'cause

82

God ain't in it." —Sarah

Forgive or Forget

I would be remiss not to mention the concept of forgiveness as an obstacle for many survivors. You've heard "forgive or forget," a popular cliche frequently heard in the church, by pastors, elders, family, etc. I am not sure who started it, but my thought is that a portion of a scripture, i.e., Matthew: 18:22 *"Jesus says we are to forgive others "seventy times seven,"* was taken out of context. This isn't the only scripture on forgiveness, but my point is that some scriptures have been twisted to pressure survivors into forgiving. However, back to my professional voice... I frequently guide clients about forgiveness on their healing journey and remind them that forgiveness is a long process. It is a personal decision on the one that has been victimized to consider the intensity of the hurt, length of relationship, and time to work through the hardship; this all must be carefully considered. It makes sense: domestic violence is not usually a single-handed issue, but continues and perpetuates for years; thus, it is unrealistic to think that forgiveness will be a short-term process. Also, forgiveness is not forgetting, meaning we don't forget the past, and we can't change it either. Yet, instead of allowing past experiences to sabotage and hurt us, we search for ways to let go of that emotional bondage. Forgiving is about freeing yourself from the hurt and anger that's weighing you down. It's about letting go of that heavy baggage so you can move forward and find your peace.

Another important concept in forgiveness is reconciliation. Forgiveness does not mean reconciliation. Reconciliation is a decision when **BOTH** the survivor and the abuser decide to restore the abusive relationship. Now, we know abusers rarely take accountability for anything. They will blame their behavior on **YOU**, alcohol, stress, mood swings, Satan, job, etc... you get my point. Also, be careful taking advice from people that may say... if you pray and forgive... God will change him...

like it's your responsibility to change their behavior and restore the relationship... umm... no, ma'am! Remember, domestic violence is a CHOICE. Unless the abuser has sought treatment from a Batterer's Intervention Program, therapy, and not anger management classes—cause domestic violence is not an anger management issue—keep moving forward.

Reconciliation requires trust and safety, which you might not get back, especially with someone who's done you wrong. Bringing an abuser back into your life can cause a major setback on your healing journey and put you at risk again. So, set boundaries to keep yourself safe.

Sis, I know we're adults, so you have every right to choose who stays in your life and who doesn't. Just know you can forgive someone in your heart, wish them well from afar, and still keep them out of your life. This way helps you stay strong and protects your mental and emotional health. Forgiveness is for you, not for them. You don't owe them a second chance at disturbing your peace. This is a part of self-compassion, or treating yourself with the same kindness and understanding that you would offer a friend who's going through the same healing.

Give yourself grace and allow yourself to feel and express your emotions without judgment. It's important to acknowledge that you're doing the best you can, even on days when it feels like you're barely holding it together. This is forgiveness too. You don't have to have everything figured out or handle every situation perfectly. Accept that setbacks are part of the healing process and that each step, no matter how small, is progress. I have forgiven my abuser, and he no longer has access to me. Therapy, prayer, and my faith helped me release him. I cannot change the past; it is a point of reference.

Here are a few affirmations I have found helpful for forgiveness:

I forgive myself for what I didn't know then.

I forgive myself for thinking it was my fault.

I forgive myself for ignoring the red flags, as I didn't know about them during the relationship.

I forgive myself for putting the needs of others before mine.

I release the pain and anger from my past, opening my heart to peace and love.

Spirituality as a source of Strength

It is evident that religious practices and beliefs can help navigate difficult life events, making spirituality, faith, and religious beliefs a source of strength and coping for Black women experiencing domestic violence. These elements often serve as a lifeline, helping us navigate the treacherous waters of domestic violence. Scholars have found a relationship between spirituality, religious involvement, religious coping, social support, and post-traumatic stress and depression in Black survivors of domestic violence. It was found that women with higher levels of spirituality and religious involvement have fewer depressive symptoms and less posttraumatic stress. In addition to that, women who were more involved in their religion had higher levels of social support. Half of the survivors you've been learning about shared that religious practices like prayer and faith were their rocks, and the other half said their personal relationships with Christ were major sources of strength. And that strength propelled them toward freedom from abuse.

Prayer and Faith

Carla talked about how faith got her through. She said, *"Just faith, just believing that God can and will change situations and circumstances. That I can go to him in prayer and know and believe that things will change has been a source of strength for me. And if it doesn't happen just the way I think it ought to happen at the time, then in my faith . . . I believe it's still for my good and when a door closes . . . there's probably something through that door that I didn't need . . . so I've always leaned on my spirituality as a foundation of faith and hope."* When it came to her marriage, she shared, *"I cried out to God to help me, because I turned to drugs and didn't want to turn into this person that I really wasn't and look up forty years later and be a broke-down drunk person. I knew there was a better way of coping with the abuse, so I definitely stepped into my faith during that time and asked for strength to stop using and get through without turning into this person that I knew wasn't me."*

Rachel had some issues with the Black church, which made her question God sometimes, but deep down, she still had that little bit of faith that things would get better. *"I was relying on God, praying . . . believing in God to spare my life. I am out of the situation now and believe that he answered my prayers and will continue to help me get back on track."*

Bobbi talked about how she prayed for the abuse to stop, and even though it didn't end right away, she kept the faith that she and her kids would be "okay." *"I kept praying for me and my kids . . . I was holding onto my faith for strength and courage."*

Vanessa shared how her prayers were answered through a church member. *"When I felt like this was the end and I couldn't go any further, do anything else . . . take the abuse anymore . . . God sent one of the sisters in my church to help me. He heard my prayers and sent her to help me ... so this gave me hope and encouragement."*

In moments of despair, faith can remind us of our worth and the divine love that surrounds us. It provides a foundation of hope and strength, offering spiritual power that helps us navigate the most challenging situations—domestic violence. Faith acts as a light, guiding us through storms. Trusting the Lord to "take the wheel" gives us the courage to take necessary steps towards safety and healing, knowing that we are never alone. The belief that God has a plan for you and that He walks with you through every trial is comforting.

Your faith is a powerful tool. It provides you with the courage to continue to seek help if we reach a roadblock and the strength to leave an abusive relationship even if it's the 6th attempt, and the hope needed to start anew. Lean into your spirituality, trust in your community, and remember that you are deserving of love, respect, and safety. Lean on scriptures that affirm your worth, strength, and value in the eyes of God, such as Psalms 147:3, "He heals the brokenhearted and binds up their wounds; Isaiah 41:10: "So do not fear, for I am with you; do not be dismayed, for I am your God. I will strengthen you and help you; I will uphold you with my righteous right hand.", and Psalms 139:13-14: "For you created my inmost being; you knit me together in my mother's womb. I praise you because I am fearfully and wonderfully made; your works are wonderful, I know that fully well."

In our faith, we grow to see that the church community is like an extended family. Members of the congregation can offer spiritual support and practical assistance when it comes to helping you find resources or providing a safe space. Their prayers and encouragement can lift you up, reinforce your faith, and give you the strength to face each day. Remember scriptures like Psalms 46:1, "God is our refuge and strength, an ever-present help in trouble," to remind yourself of the divine support available to you. Reflect on 2 Timothy 1:7, "For God has not given us a spirit of fear, but of power and of love and of a sound mind." These words are meant to uplift and remind you of your inner strength.

Last, Remember Isaiah 41:10, "So do not fear, for I am with you; do not be dismayed, for I am your God. I will strengthen you and help you; I will uphold you with my righteous right hand." This scripture reminds us that God is always with us, offering strength and support. Reflect on Philippians 4:13, "I can do all things through Christ who strengthens me." Let these words empower you to take steps toward safety, healing and empowerment. Check out the resource provided that highlights a breakdown of frequently utilized biblical scriptures often used to keep survivors in abusive relationships.

Relationship with Christ

April talked about how being tight with Jesus and filled with the Holy Spirit and trusting Him to look out for her and her kids. This connection gave her strength and hope. She shared, "*My relationship with Christ and being filled with the Holy Spirit and trusting him that he's going to take care of me and my children, gave me strength and hope.*" She recalled a time when the Holy Spirit gave her a clear sign about her husband's behavior, which gave her the power to leave her abusive marriage. She said, "*There were times when I would wake up in the middle of the night and God would reveal things to me concerning my husband. . . . for instance, one night, the Holy Spirit told me to go look in the closet . . . specifically where and when I went. . . . there was pornography and all kinds of craziness . . . so I started praying and asking the Holy Spirit how to address it. I never searched through my ex-husband's things, so I know it was the Holy Spirit that revealed the stuff to me. I can't really deny that God got me through because he is the only one that got me through.*"

April also elaborated on how her relationship with Christ provided clarity on Christ's principles for marriage. "*My relationship with Christ and being filled with the Holy Spirit, I knew that God would take care of me and my children. I deepened my relationship with Christ and had developed more insight into God's way of how husbands and wives should treat each other. As a result, I had realized that my marriage was not a reflection of God's desire for husbands and wives. I never thought I would be in a shelter, and I know God has me here for a reason... to bless and encourage other women. I finally made peace with the process of gaining control of her life and healing simultaneously.*" —April

Sami shared: "*When you're with God and have a relationship with Christ . . . you feel like he can get you through things, even when it's hard and everything you learn in Church. . . . like, he won't put more on you than you can bear, and sometimes it feels like it, but you have to have that faith that he is going to see you through and that you're going to come out better than what you started. I prayed about my situation . . . and was scared during the abuse . . . but I just felt like with God . . . it would get better. I'm still scared with this new start . . . but I know he's with me."*

Sarah said: *"My entire spirituality is based on the fact that someone suffered so much more than I could ever suffer in order for me to exist. So, that has given me so much strength during this process."*

Another woman mentioned that along with her relationship with Christ, her religious upbringing gave her another source of strength, and together, they made her strong. Tina shared: *"Because I was raised in the Church and I knew the Lord and still know him today . . . I would always talk to him. I know he saved me from death. . . . I always called on him and he's never failed me. . . . He was always a source of strength for me, always."*

"My sense of spirituality was based on the fact that Christ had suffered so much more than I could ever suffer. He suffered on the cross in order for me to exist... so this has given me strength when I feel like I can't make it... but optimistic that God would make a way as I continued to heal." —Sara

Some of the women said that stepping back from the Black church allowed them to develop a personal relationship with Christ instead of relying solely on what pastors and church leaders interpreted and this helped them cope better. Those who turned to drugs and alcohol realized that these unhealthy coping strategies were counterproductive, and God provided them an escape. By relying on prayer, faith, and a personal relationship with Christ, they began to challenge oppressive biblical teachings and moved towards self-respect and healing.

Tina's admiration for the Church led her to them for assistance regardless of the expected conflicting statements and interactions she witnessed growing up. *"I've always been a member of a Black church, and it seems like there's just something about it . . . something about being around your people that feels good. Because I was raised in the Church and I knew the Lord and still know him today . . . I would always talk to him. I know he saved me from death. . . . I always called on him and he's never failed me. . . . He was always a source of strength for me, always."* —Tina

As a result of achieving this profound clarity, she had realized that her marriage was not a reflection of God's desire for husbands and wives. Thus, she was finally at peace with the process of gaining control of her life and healing simultaneously.

"I never thought I would be in a shelter, and I know God has me here for a reason...to bless and encourage other women." —April

In wrapping things up, it's clear that faith, spirituality, and religion play powerful roles in the healing journey for Black women survivors. It has also played a pivotal role in my healing journey. As I reflect, I didn't seek guidance from a pastor regarding my abusive relationship because I was an emerging adult when I experienced abuse and did not think about it. Also, I hadn't yet joined a church during my undergrad days. However, I have leaned heavily on my pastor for other hardships in my life, such as grief, job transitions, etc. In addition, my personal relationship with Christ strengthened my discernment in relationships and all areas of my life. For example, I prayed for clarity about some relationships, and my lens was open to repeated relational patterns and things about myself that required healing. It has been a game changer.

See, these spiritual elements aren't just parts of my identity or your identity; they shape how we all navigate and overcome the hardships we face. For many, faith and spirituality offer a source of strength, hope, community, and support. It is what keeps them going when everything else seems hopeless and what helps them find the courage to take that first step towards freedom. At the same time, it's vital to recognize the challenges spirituality can bring, especially when traditional beliefs clash with the need to escape abusive situations. Understanding this intersection is key to finding a path that honors both our spiritual selves and our need for safety and well-being. As we move forward, embracing this complexity can empower us to heal, grow, and reclaim our lives with a sense of wholeness and peace.

Reflection Prompts

1. How has your faith or spiritual beliefs provided you with strength, comfort, or guidance during your relationship and healing journey?

2. In what ways have your spiritual beliefs or faith posed challenges in your decision to leave an abusive relationship?

3. How has your faith community impacted your experience and choices regarding domestic violence? (think about the advice, support or judgment you may have received from faith leaders, etc.)

4. What spiritual practices have you found helpful to navigate your mental health and healing?

Keeping the Faith: Guidance for Christian Women Facing Abuse

For Christian victims of sexual and domestic violence, the Bible can be a barrier to freedom...

"This is just my cross to bear." When Christ told his followers to "pick up your cross and follow me" (Mt. 10:38, 16:24; Luke 9:23), he meant that his followers may have to suffer if they follow in his footsteps. It is dangerous to speak out against injustice, to be in ministry in broken communities, or to speak God's word of peace in a violent and power-hungry world. Jesus was prepared to suffer in order to make God's kingdom of peace and justice a reality. But the suffering that domestic violence inflicts is different. It is imposed from without, rather than freely chosen by the victim. Instead of establishing God's Kingdom, the suffering of domestic violence is in opposition to God's kingdom, where peace and joy abound. God does not mean for anyone to suffer abuse.

"Christ suffered for me, now it's my turn to suffer for Christ." Paul said that Christ died for our sins, not so that we may continue to suffer, but that we may have eternal life (Rom. 6:23). The writer of Hebrews says, "For by a single offering he has perfected for all time those who are sanctified." (Heb. 10:14). Suffering for the sake of suffering is not redemptive. Jesus has justified and redeemed us.

"I made a vow before God. What God has joined, let no one tear asunder." (Matt. 19:6). The covenant of marriage is "torn asunder" by the abuser's violence, not by the victim's need to speak the truth about the violence. God does not intend for the marriage covenant to be a place of violence, verbal abuse, or victimization.

"I was taught to turn the other cheek and to forgive 7 x 70."

Jesus taught us not to return evil for evil, to pray for our enemies, and not to be vindictive. But this does not mean that Christians are to be punching bags. Paul says, "hate what is evil; cling to what is good... never avenge yourselves, but leave it to the wrath of God; for it is written: 'Vengeance is mine, I will repay, says the lord'" (Rom. 12:17, 19). Abusers are subject to God's judgment, and their behavior is condemned by God. Forgiveness must be predicated on the batterer's repentance, and repentance means changed behavior, not just saying, "I'm sorry, honey."

"Women should be subject to their husbands." The Bible says that the husband and the wife should "be subject to one another out of reverence to Christ." (Eph. 5:21). Within that context, Paul goes on to say that "women should be subject to their husbands," but also that "the husband is the head of the wife as Christ is the head of the Church, his body and himself its Savior" (Eph. 5:22-23). Remember that, as the head of the Church, Christ served, nourished, and cherished the church, and even died for its sake. Christ would never do anything to abuse or oppress the church. Neither should husbands abuse or oppress their wives. Rather, the two are to live together in mutual respect and love. As the writer of Colossians says, "Husbands, love your wives, and do not be harsh with them" (Col. 3:19).

All people are "a temple of the Holy Spirit." If anyone destroys God's temple, God will destroy him" (1 Cor. 3:16-17). We are all precious and valued children of God. We are made in God's likeness, and God's spirit dwells in us. God never wills for one of His children to be abused. Abusers stand against God's judgment.

"Jesus came to give life, and to give it abundantly" (John 10:10). God's will for us is not that we merely survive from day to day, wondering when this nightmare will be over, but that we have a life that is rewarding, joyful, faithful, and fulfilling. God wants us to grow spiritually, and be able to respond to God's call in our lives. Physical, mental, verbal, financial, and spiritual abuse undermine a life of faith.

God calls people of faith out of oppression and into the Promised Land. When the people of Israel were in slavery in Egypt, God heard their cries for help (Ex. 3:7-9) and came to their aid. God delivered them from their oppression "with a mighty hand" (Ex. 3:39), and led them through the Wilderness to the Promised Land. God stands on the side of the oppressed, and is active in human lives to move people from oppression to freedom. God hears the cries of domestic violence victims too, and walks with them towards safety and freedom.

God will not abandon us. People of the Bible knew what it was to have their friend, their intimate partner, turn against them. The Psalms are a great resource for victims who are feeling abandoned (Ps. 22) or distressed (Ps. 55, 120). However, the Psalmist also speaks of the comfort of God's presence (Ps. 22, 91, 118) and God's guidance on the journey toward freedom, (Ps. 22, 107).

This has been provided by Safe Havens Interfaith Partnership Against Domestic Violence using material from Marie Fortune's Keeping the Faith: Guidance for Christian Women Facing Abuse.

Chapter 5: The Path to Healing: A Journey to Discovery

"Because coming home to ourselves is where true healing begins..." —Sonia Sanchez

I believe that everyone deserves a safe, healthy relationship free of violence. However, the most important relationship is the one you have with yourself. Therefore, healing begins by turning inward. What I mean is that after you are out of survivor mode, you can breathe a little and take steps towards peace and a life without violence. That step starts with your motivation and commitment to being a better woman, mother, sister, faith leader, etc. It is a journey to discover how childhood connects to your adult life—why you do what you do, why you think the way you think, and ultimately, who you are. Please keep in mind that making a commitment can be overwhelming and can be due to a number of things, such as finances for therapy or job flexibility to attend appointments, or could you just be depleted from being in a flight or fight mode. Remember, everyone's situation is different, so I encourage you to practice self-compassion and exchange self-doubt for empowerment. You can do this. Healing is not linear, and this chapter provides tools and insights to help you navigate the emotional, mental, and physical journey of healing. It emphasizes stages of trauma recovery, barriers to healing, and healing practices that nourish your well-being.

Healing from trauma can feel weird, difficult, and uncomfortable at first, but also rewarding. It's about reclaiming your life. According to Trauma Expert, Dr. Judith Herman, trauma recovery is thought to occur in three stages: 1. Safety & Stabilization, 2. Trauma Reprocessing/Mourning, and 3. Reconnection/Integration.

Safety & Stabilization

The hardest part of healing is safety because as a result of the trauma you've endured, you don't feel safe in your body, environment, or relationships. And, when you lose your sense of safety, it is difficult to process your trauma. So, the first step is feeling safe and stable. This involves creating a safe living environment, developing coping skills to manage intense emotions, and establishing routines. As I mentioned earlier, I started trauma therapy in 2020, and I didn't realize I was getting triggered. I felt off, out of control, and unable to manage intrusive thoughts and emotions. Connecting with a therapist helped me develop coping tools to manage triggers and regain a sense of control and calm in my life.

Trauma & Reprocessing/Mourning

In the second stage, you start to process and make sense of your traumatic experiences. This often involves talking about the trauma with a therapist or in a safe, supportive setting. The goal is to confront and work through the painful memories. This is important because confronting the trauma helps to integrate your experience into your life, rather than having them remain as isolated, painful memories. It allows for the release of emotions that were previously suppressed or overwhelming. Also, in this second stage is an opportunity to recognize what was lost as a result of domestic violence. This can look like grieving the loss of the relationship or relationships that were created as a result that you may no longer have and grieving an old version of yourself. For me, EMDR and brainspotting sessions provided space for reprocessing traumatic experiences. It was a catalyst for discovering myself and why I do what I do.

Integration/Reconnection

This final stage is about reconnecting with everyday life and the world. You begin to build a new sense of self and find a new meaning and purpose. This might involve developing new relationships and engaging in activities you enjoy or setting new life goals. This stage helps you move forward and recognize that you are not defined by your TRAUMA. It is one part of you, not all of you. It's about creating a fulfilling and connected life, where the trauma is a part of your history, but does not dominate your present or future. Essentially, a resurrection.

During the healing journey, there are a lot of unknowns. Like how long will this take, will therapy help, etc.But I figured I had more to gain than lose... so I proceeded forward. My turning point during my healing journey came during therapy. I was there for a different family issue, but through that, I saw the cycle of abuse in my family clearly. Self-awareness became my ticket out of that abusive relationship and the key to healing. I was blessed to have the resources for therapy and to start a more empowered life. Part of my healing led me to discuss with my mother her reasons for staying in an abusive marriage: to keep the family together and ensure her daughters had a father around. I was happy and grateful that she was open to this conversation, as it was the catalyst to the journey of healing the younger version of me. As for my father, he passed away before my healing journey began. My therapist encouraged me to learn about his childhood and parents to gain a better understanding of him. Gathering this information was very helpful and initiated the forgiveness process. A few days before he passed, he apologized to me for how he treated my mother and said she is a good woman. Not only did he change his behavior, but he expressed remorse. Therefore, I challenged you to broach your experiences with your parents. Do so with the intention to share and without expectations for them to apologize. They may not have capacity to apologize or know how to do so; this is for you and your healing.

Healing can also be challenging when you don't fully understand your trauma, and you might find yourself in similar situations over and over again. For instance, you run back to what feels comfortable because anything new feels weird. Something new can be as simple as experiencing a day where you don't hear anyone yelling or even silence. Constant noise, chaos, or dysfunction can feel normal if that is all you know. When you finally remove yourself from that environment, ten minutes of silence may hurt your ears. I know that seems weird, but it happens. Breaking the cycle involves a deep journey of self-discovery and healing. You need to recognize the patterns in your life and understand the root causes of your pain. This is because we must learn from the cycle to avoid repeating the same behavior. Now let me run this back: after I was out of the abusive relationship, I thought I was ready for "love again." Whew, I was so wrong. I repeatedly got into unhealthy relationships; they weren't abusive; just unhealthy. For example, I found myself attached to guys that weren't emotionally available, separated, in situationships, or struggling with their mental health. I didn't realize that these were red flags; basically, they were not healthy or ready for a relationship. But GOD, when I finally said YES to me... the shift happened ... the ugly cry and all... I told myself with some doubt that I was worthy of healing and welcomed singleness with a new perspective.

With that being said, the path to healing starts with you; the moment you decide to say yes to yourself. It starts when you recognize that your well-being and happiness are worth prioritizing, even after years of silence. By picking up this book, you are saying YES to you. Also, it can mean your journey to healing has either started or it's ongoing. Each word you have read has now become a part of your healing and thriving process.

Finding your voice after being oppressed and silenced for long is a powerful act of self-love and courage. It's about reclaiming your identity, setting boundaries, and allowing yourself to express your true thoughts and feelings. This journey to discovery isn't always easy, but each step you take towards embracing your voice and saying yes to your own needs is a step towards healing and inner peace.

Keep in mind that healing from trauma is a gradual and deeply personal process. It involves acknowledging the wounds and pain, understanding its impact, and slowly working through the emotions that have been buried for so long. Also, it involves realizing that once your body is out of flight or fight mode, you crave a lot of rest. In addition, this journey is often marked by moments of vulnerability, where confronting the past can feel overwhelming. However, it is through this process that true healing begins. As you allow yourself to feel and process these emotions, you start to release the hold that trauma has had on you. You release the control that the abuser had on you—that emotional control. You know "out the relationship," but still in bondage. Each step forward, no matter how small, is a victory in reclaiming your life and finding strength in your resilience. As mentioned, the process is ongoing, but with patience, self-compassion, and support, it leads to profound transformation and renewal. So, as you continue on this path, it's important to recognize the signs of progress and celebrate your growth. I want to share some indicators that you are healing,so you can see how far you've come and find encouragement to keep moving forward. Please note this list is not an exhaustive list of what to expect when healing from trauma. Everyone is different; your journey is unique to you, your identities, and experiences:

1. You've acknowledged that what you have experienced is a trauma. Remember, you can't heal what you don't feel.

2. You are able to name your feelings. You begin feeling your emotions rather than suppressing or minimizing them. For instance, you allow yourself to cry.

3. You are more in tune with how your body responds. For instance, you are aware of triggers and how to manage them. Traumatic experiences can take a toll on the body, when your flight/fight/freeze/fawn system is activated.

4. You are not as emotionally reactive (blow up, pop off on someone) or you respond rather than react.

5. You are able to talk about the trauma.

6. You no longer blame yourself for what happened.

7. You can set and practice boundaries.

8. You can enjoy time alone.

9. You are okay with being misunderstood.

10. You are aware of how your past trauma shows up presently.

While there are signs of progress in your healing journey, there are also indicators that suggest you may need to focus more on certain aspects of your recovery. These signs can serve as gentle reminders that healing is not always linear and that it's okay to seek additional support or take more time for yourself. Recognizing these signals is a crucial part of ensuring that your journey remains healthy and balanced. Again, please note this list is not an exhaustive list of what to expect when you're healing slowly from trauma. Everyone is different; your journey is unique to you, your identities, and experiences:

1. Struggling with accepting your experience is traumatic.

2. Inability to revisit the trauma in therapy. Any reminder(s) of the trauma can lead to increased symptoms of depression, anxiety, anger, resentment, suicidal ideations.

3. Attached to abusive people. Not all people that experience domestic violence will cling to abusive people, but many survivors find themselves in similar unhealthy relationships. We attach to people and behaviors that we are familiar with. Anything new, such as healthy relationships feel weird.

4. You are okay with ignoring triggers.

5. Putting others's needs before your own to avoid conflict.

6. Constant feeling of being on edge.

7. Always expecting the worse to happen.

8. Using substances to cope with pain.

9. Socially withdrawing yourself but feeling lonely.

10. Reliving traumatic events through dreams or random thoughts.

Barriers and challenges of Healing

A big part of trauma recovery is understanding that healing is a choice. Healing is like walking through quicksand, if you stop moving, you may sink. Yes, you go under as you visit the darkest parts of your experiences, but as you keep going you will come out on the other side a lot stronger then when you first started. Starting over after domestic violence is tough, especially for Black women who face unique challenges on this journey to healing. The path to recovery is rarely straightforward, often marked by issues such as financial demands, the responsibilities of single parenthood, and the complexities of dating while healing.

Many of us Black women are walking through that quicksand with kids, careers and dreams, and sometimes that brings its own sets of challenges and barriers to healing. Balancing work and kids while trying to heal from trauma can be overwhelming, it makes the healing process a little more complex. Some are transitioning into the workforce in order to leave abuse. A full-time job or demanding work schedule means you only have a little time for self-reflection, therapy, and healing activities. I know meeting deadlines and managing workloads can cause a different kind of emotional exhaustion and can make it hard to prioritize mental health. At the same time, parenting duties, especially for our little babies, require constant attention and energy. We have to acknowledge the emotional demands of children too, so much that the need for personal time we need can get overlooked. Juggling these responsibilities can leave us vulnerable and open to past abusers or new abusers coming to the "rescue."

First, let's talk about the financial barriers. According to the National Coalition Against Domestic Violence, financial barriers are a significant challenge for survivors when leaving abusive situations. Between 21% and 60% of survivors stay in or return to abusive relationships primarily due to financial dependence on their abuser. This statistic highlights how economic abuse and financial insecurity can trap survivors in dangerous situations, making it even more difficult for them to seek safety and rebuild their lives. With that being said, leaving an abusive relationship often means starting from scratch. Many Black women leave without the financial resources they need to start over. The survivors that you have learned about were homeless and struggled with basic needs such as food and clothing. The cost of housing, childcare, attorney fees, loss of income due to attending court hearings, relocation fees, and daily expenses can be overwhelming, especially when you've been financially dependent on your partner. This can create a cycle of stress and anxiety, making it hard to focus on healing. You might find yourself working multiple jobs or relying on community resources just to make ends meet. The financial strain can feel suffocating, but remember, every small step towards financial independence is a victory.

Next, there's the reality of single parenthood. Being a single mother means you're juggling all the responsibilities of parenthood alone. You're the provider, the nurturer, the disciplinarian, and the comforter. It's a lot. The demands of raising children on your own can leave little time for self-care and healing. We know kids need stability and support, which means putting their needs ahead of our own. Finding a balance between taking care of our children and finding time to heal can feel impossible. Yet, it's crucial to carve out moments for yourself, even if it's just a few minutes each day. Your well-being directly impacts your ability to care for your children.

Then, there's the challenge of dating while in the process of healing. After experiencing domestic violence, opening up to someone new can be terrifying. Trust has been shattered, and the wounds are raw. Also, the thought of being vulnerable again can be paralyzing. That's why it's crucial to take time to understand your needs and desires in a relationship. Prioritize your emotional well-being and set clear boundaries. Here are a few things to consider before stepping into the dating world again.

Give it a Year or So

Taking a year or more off before entering another relationship can be incredibly beneficial for several reasons. This time allows you time to process some of the initial grief and emotional wounds of your past relationship, helping to rebuild your sense of self and confidence. It gives you the space to reflect on your experiences, understand what you truly need and want in a partner, and establish healthy boundaries. Additionally, this period of self-care and growth ensures that when you do decide to start dating again, you're doing so from a place of strength and clarity, rather than from a place of unresolved pain, loneliness or fear. By giving yourself this time, you're prioritizing your emotional well-being and setting the foundation for a healthier, more fulfilling future relationship. Essentially, a form of self-love.

Identify Your Triggers

Understand what situations or behaviors might remind you of past trauma. Knowing your triggers helps you manage your reactions and communicate your needs to a potential partner.

Know What You Are Looking For

Be clear about what you want in a relationship. This clarity helps you avoid settling for less and ensures you find someone who respects and values you. For instance, identify your deal breakers.

Consider Compatibility with Trauma and Triggers

Make sure both you and your potential partner can handle each other's trauma and triggers. Open communication about past experiences and coping mechanisms is important for mutual understanding and support.

Evaluate the Relationship's Tools for Healing

Check if the relationship has the necessary tools to navigate healing, such as good communication, empathy, and patience. These tools are essential for maintaining a healthy and supportive relationship.

Reflect on Self-Learning.

Consider what you've learned about yourself since your previous relationship. Self-awareness is key to growth and helps you avoid repeating past mistakes.

Recognize Red and Green Flags.

Be real about recognizing signs of healthy and unhealthy behavior. This awareness helps you make informed decisions and ensures you're not ignoring potential warning signs and repeating cycles. Revisit the power and control wheel for red flags. On the contrary, green flags are positive indicators that a relationship has the potential to be safe and healthy. Some examples include respecting boundaries, honesty, respect, shared values, and conflict resolution skills. Check out my feature in Self-Magazine for more information.

https://www.self.com/story/relationship-green-flags

Also, keep in mind since healing is ongoing, you can date while healing, but by taking these steps, you can approach dating with a stronger sense of self and a clearer understanding of what you need in a partner. Remember, your healing journey is unique, and it's important to prioritize your well-being above all else.

Healing Practices

Self-care has become a popular buzzword. Especially since the pandemic, you have seen TikTok videos, reels, and memes on "self-care" activities. The way I approach self-care and help clients with this notion is to consider self-care as activities you do on a consistent basis to maintain optimal mental health. Things you do to avoid feeling like you're reaching a breaking point and must take a vacation to feel better. Afterall, everyone can't afford trips, spa days, or brunches, but we can at least commit to taking steps to care for our well-being. That could be listening to your favorite worship song to recenter yourself or drinking more water. I would like to share some of the healing practices that have been most meaningful to me.

Counseling

Counseling provides a safe space where you can express your feelings, work through trauma, and start to heal. It's a place where you can be heard without judgment and where you can begin to understand and process your experiences. Going to counseling is an achievable step in your self-care journey. It's all about prioritizing your well-being and reclaiming your life. Think of a counselor as someone who can help lay out a guided path to discovering your strength and self-worth. A skilled therapist can help you navigate the complex emotions and challenges that come with healing from abuse. During sessions, you'll be equipped with coping strategies and tools to help rebuild your confidence and set healthy boundaries. As I mentioned in Chapter 4, one important tool for helping to reframe negative beliefs is using CBT techniques. Here's another example: *"I stayed too long in the abusive relationship, so it's my fault I was hurt;* healthier perspective: *"I did what I could to survive in a difficult situation, and choosing to leave was an act of strength and courage."* I say that all to say that taking the steps to seek professional help is a declaration of self-love. It's saying you deserve peace, happiness, and a life free from fear. Remember, it's okay to ask for help and lean on others as you heal. I delved deeper into phases of counseling in Chapter 6.

Prayer

Prayer offers a moment of peace, a chance to connect with a higher power, and a way to express your deepest fears and hopes. When everything feels out of control, prayer can ground you, helping you find a sense of stability and inner strength. It doesn't require anything but a quiet moment, whether you're in your bedroom, taking a walk, or even sitting in your car. Through prayer, you can seek guidance, find solace, and draw strength to move forward. It's a way to regain your power and remind yourself that you are worthy of love, peace, and happiness. Prayer helps me feel close to God, it is one of the ways I stay connected to him.

Exercise

Exercising is more than just a way to stay fit; it's a way to regain your body, mind and spirit. Your body is a house that often carries the weight of that pain. One of my favorite books, The Body Keeps Score by Bessel van Kolk explains how trauma affects the body and mind and how it can be healed. Remember in Chapter 3, we cover how trauma can cause physical manifestations such as chronic pain, fatigue or immune problems because our bodies remember traumatic experiences. Therefore, exercise can help you release that tension in our muscles and joints to feel strong and empowered again. Whether it's taking a brisk walk in the park, joining a dance class, or finding your flow with yoga, moving your body can lift your mood and help clear your mind. It's not about hitting the gym every day or pushing yourself to the limit; it's about finding what feels good and works for you.

Mindfulness and Yoga

Mindfulness and yoga practices offer more than just physical benefits; they can help you heal emotionally and mentally. Mindfulness is all about being present in the moment and paying attention to your thoughts and feelings without judgment. Especially after being in flight or fight mode for so long, it is difficult to be still and pay attention to your body, senses, and thoughts. So, mindfulness can help you regain control over your mind and emotions. Also, when you are mindful, you are more attuned to your body and able to manage triggers. Simple practices like mindful breathing, meditation, or even just taking a few moments to focus on the things around you can make a big difference. Staying present can reduce anxiety, manage stress, and help build a sense of inner peace. Some of my favorite apps for meditation are Liberate, Insight Timer, Exhale, Calm, and Headspace.

Yoga, on the other hand, combines physical movement with breathwork and can help reconnect with your body. Through gentle stretches, poses, and deep breathing, yoga helps release tension, build strength, and improve flexibility. More importantly, it fosters a sense of self-compassion and acceptance, which is essential for healing. There are many variations of yoga: Yin, Restorative, Vinyasa and Trauma-Informed. My favorites are restorative and trauma informed yoga. I like restorative yoga because it is slow-paced. Trauma-informed yoga is a safe and gentle way that considers the needs of people that have experienced traumatic experiences. Keep in mind that any form of movement

Nutrition

Nutrition is not just about eating right; it's about nurturing yourself inside and out. You can start with small changes. Incorporate more fruits and vegetables into your meals, and make sure you're getting enough protein to keep your energy up. Hydrate regularly, aiming for plenty of water throughout the day. These small steps can make a big difference in how you feel physically and emotionally. Did you know that 90% of serotonin—a neurotransmitter, also known as the happy hormone or feel good chemical—is made in the stomach? It helps control the mood and other bodily functions such as sleep, memory, and digestion. When your serotonin levels are normal, you feel happier, calmer, focused, or more stable. When they are low, you may feel down, in a funk, which is associated with depression. So, what you eat matters. By prioritizing nutrition, you're not just feeding your body; you're also feeding your soul, empowering yourself to heal and thrive. And remember it's okay to seek help. Whether it's consulting with a nutritionist or joining a support group, reaching out for guidance can provide you with the tools and encouragement you need to stay on track.

Advocacy

By speaking out, sharing your story, and helping others who are in similar situations, you reclaim your voice and power. Getting involved in advocacy allows you to connect with a community of survivors and allies who understand your experiences. This sense of belonging can be incredibly healing. Advocacy can take many forms, from community outreach to volunteering with domestic violence agencies or writing letters of advocacy to media outlets, newspapers, or elected officials for domestic violence awareness. Advocacy can provide a sense of purpose but also offer an opportunity to contribute to a cause that is meaningful to you. By helping others, you can find strength in your journey and transform your experiences into a force for positive change. I have found that sharing my story is not only empowering and therapeutic but liberating. One of my proudest moments is when I wrote a letter of advocacy to the American Counseling Association to create an Intimate Partner Violence (IPV) Interest Network Group for counselors and students with shared interests and concerns about IPV. This was so important to me because not only was I advocating for my colleagues, but I was advocating for survivors, and most importantly, me.

Overall, remember there is no time limit to the healing journey, and it's important to take small steps, celebrate milestones, and find moments of peace and self-compassion along the way. What I have learned and still learning is that healing is ongoing, challenging, yet rewarding, liberating and sacred. It's an investment in yourself. Healing requires time—time to reflect, time to feel, and time to grow. Yes, you must invest in yourself and pay attention to your needs and honor the process every step of the way.

When you invest in yourself, you're doing more than just surviving—you're reclaiming your power and redefining your life on your own terms. You're giving yourself permission to prioritize your well-being, to put yourself first, and to say, "I matter." When you pay attention to your needs, you dedicate yourself to your healing. Every moment spent nurturing your spirit is building a stronger and more resilient you. So, take the time you need to pour into yourself, and trust that with each step, you're moving closer to the freedom and joy you deserve. Your journey is yours, and it's worth every ounce of energy, love, and care you give it.

Reflection Prompts

1. What does healing mean to you? What does healing look like for you? What would it feel like: mentally, physically, emotionally, relationally?

2. Reflect on some important Black women in your life; how did you see them engage in self-care? What does self-care mean to you?

3. Who taught you how to heal? How will you help others heal?

CHAPTER: 6. A TRIBE CALLED SUPPORT

"There is Healing in Community." —Audre Lorde

As a lover of all things hip hop, my support system - my tribe - shares that same love. Back in my undergraduate days, they were the ones who stood by me through every exam, heartbreak, and breakthrough. One of our favorite ways to connect was through meetups where we listened to A Tribe Called Quest and opened up about the highs and lows of life. When my abusive relationship ended, I didn't realize that this fellowship was a form of healing and support - but looking back, it was exactly what I needed. After an abusive relationship, survivors are in a very frail and delicate state. Especially after an agonizing decision that can take years to make to leave the relationship. Likewise, I was in a very fragile position, and spending time with my support system was actually rewiring healthy neural pathways or connections in my brain. Healing is amplified in safe, affirming spaces. This chapter emphasizes the importance of healthy connections with friends, family, counselors, and spiritual communities. It offers guidance on how to find and cultivate your "tribe".

What I have learned from my experience, therapy, and research is that healthy relationships and connections, whether it's platonic or romantic, can heal trauma. We are relational beings, wired for connection; we aren't designed to be isolated from others. While trauma disrupts connections, healthy relationships can heal trauma. One cultural framework I use in my work is Relational-Cultural Theory, or RCT. Simply put, RCT is based on the idea that healing happens through healthy, supportive relationships - not in isolation. It teaches that we grow and heal best when we feel connected, seen, and valued by others. For me, my healing began with my tribe - those friends from my undergrad years, a very small circle that showed up, listened, and reminded me of my worth. Spending time with my tribe allowed me to see that despite how isolated I felt at times, I was not alone. Every opportunity in communion with my tribe provided comfort, solace, and encouragement. I felt inspired to stay focused on my healing journey and rebuild my self worth. I felt okay with sharing parts of my story at my own time and pace without judgment. I was slowly transforming from disempowered to empowered. My healing began with my tribe. That's why it's so important to surround yourself with a supportive community as you move through your healing journey.

Finding Community

When we think of community, sometimes we initially imagine a group of people around you or living in close proximity. But that's not necessarily true. Community looks different for everyone. For survivors, a supportive community is one that reminds you of your worth, celebrates your courage to leave, and listens with love versus judgment. This is necessary because for many, the abuse doesn't just end after you leave the relationship. I wish it did, but honestly, it doesn't. Yes, sis, even after you leave, the abusers may continue their control by harassing you at work, using your children as tools for manipulation, attempting to damage your reputation with family and friends, or even by filing legal actions against you as a form of intimidation. Having a supportive community complements your healing and can include - but is not limited to trusted family members, close friends, counselors, faith leaders, supportive groups, counselors, advocates and survivor support networks.

How to identify your tribe?

Look for people that are non-judgmental, trustworthy, supportive, and willing to allow you to make decisions that are best for you in your healing journey. Afterall, you know your situation better than anyone. A community of non-judgmental care is vital to healing. It fosters holistic well-being and offers great benefits to improve your mental, physical, and spiritual health. As a result, you'll be more likely to reach out when you're having a tough moment and more comfortable opening up. Also, you will be less likely to be subjected to criticism. With that being said, even if your community doesn't understand domestic violence, a non-judgmental community allows them to not only support you but learn about the many facets of power and control.

Here are some examples of nonjudgmental statements:

- I don't know what it's like to experience domestic violence, but you deserve to be treated with respect and dignity.

- I respect your decision on how you decide to proceed.

- I value you as a person and am happy to support your safety plan.

On the flip side, some people we may want to include in our tribe, i.e., family, friends, faith community, are not always the best choice. For example, people on the outside of your relationship have this notion that you can just leave the relationship, but they don't know the full story of what you're experiencing. They're quite judgmental and assert their opinion on what you should or shouldn't do. Also, it's quite hurtful when people you love offer unsolicited advice on something they don't know about when you need unconditional love and support. This can hinder your healing. In addition, judgment exacerbates the shame and guilt you already had from being in an abusive relationship. In other words, you are further traumatized and victimized, making it difficult to overcome your trauma. Whenever I heard a judgmental statement, I was triggered, and it took time for me to accept that they didn't understand domestic violence. If you find people in your community advising you to go back to the relationship, or suggest it isn't that bad or utilize religious cliches such as pray and stay or God hates divorce, they are disqualified for admission into your tribe. Keep them at a distance; so far until you have built confidence in your decision-leaving process.

Here are some example judgmental statements:

- Why did you stay so long? What were you doing? What were you wearing? (Victim blaming)
- The kids need their father.
- Y'all need to go to marriage counseling.
- There are two sides to the story.
- I've never seen them be abusive to you when I'm around y'all.
- I would've never stayed that long (shaming opinion).

A primary reason people are judgmental is probably that they lack understanding about domestic violence. Black women take pride in everything we do, and we ain't broadcasting our stuff, let alone abuse. So, due to still a lot of stigma associated with domestic violence, our community just doesn't get it. If you find yourself with more judgmental people than nonjudgmental people in your tribe, you can tell them how to support you and/or have a conversation with them to help them better understand your experiences.

Here are a few statements and strategies to navigate judgmental people while protecting your peace and progress:

- I'm happy with my decision, THANKS!
- I'm okay with the pace things are going with my healing journey, thank you.
- I would rather you listen without feedback, thanks!
- Set boundaries without apology
- Ground yourself in your truth: Remind yourself that others' opinions don't define your reality. Keep 1 or 2 affirmations that center your truth and experience: "I know what I experienced: I know my story".

Remember, it is okay to distance yourself from judgmental

people. At this stage in your healing journey, you need people for strength, support and encouragement.

It is critical to have people in your tribe that are trustworthy and supportive. Especially after your trust has been shattered from the abusive relationship, you don't know who to trust. My faith and trust in people and relationships was little to none. Finding people that I could trust with my experience and trust that they weren't going back to my ex to tell him what I said or try to get his side of the story was vital to my healing journey. The last thing I needed was someone trying to be a mediator to rekindle the relationship. So, I found people that kept my situation confidential, didn't minimize my experiences, and prioritized my safety and well-being. As I mentioned earlier, a few family members, along with my sorority line-sisters and best friend in college, set the foundation of my support system.

As I felt more comfortable and less anxious about being judged, I shared more of my experiences. However, there were people in my community that I knew would be supportive but also attempt to retaliate against the abuser. For example, my parents. I never told my father, and I told my mother years later. I was faced with this dilemma: tell my parents or protect my abuser. I chose the latter because I was conditioned to looking out for him versus my needs. Also, it was less risky; in other words, protecting my abuser reduced the likelihood of more abuse. My community organically evolved as I continued to progress in my healing. I am at peace with the fact my father never knew what happened, and my mother accepted my process to disclose when I was ready. My faith in making decisions about my healing journey gradually increased as I found my voice and extended grace to myself. Currently, as I share more of my story with people, I have mentally rehearsed what I will say if I'm judged or what they will think of me. These thoughts still come up, but I have learned to speak my truth and not look back or worry about what others will think; afterall, they haven't experienced it.

Support groups

Support groups, whether virtual or in person, are an added bonus to your healing journey. While I've never attended a support group for abuse, I attended a grief support group after the loss of my father. It was comforting to be in community with others that had experienced a loss. A support group among people with similar experiences offered me comfort and healing. It complimented my healing journey. Not everyone had lost a parent, but the common theme was grief after the death of a loved one. Similarly, domestic violence support groups provide a safe, caring and nonjudgmental environment for survivors that have experienced abuse.

Because domestic violence trauma affects so many areas of your life, support groups offer a valuable space to express emotions and develop coping skills for challenges like managing triggers and practicing assertive communication. They also offer practical tools and resources to assist in recovery, as well as increased self awareness and patterns of behavior. As Black women, we don't like airing our "dirty laundry" with people. Our culture has conditioned us to keep things to ourselves, essentially suffering in silence. We think we will be judged. On the flip side, if we decide to do it, we at least want to be in community with other Black women; it feels safe and affirming to be in community with our sistas. So, we are reluctant and don't trust these spaces where there is little to no representation of Black women. I get it; trust me; I do. However, support groups help alleviate feelings of isolation and loneliness. An affirming space to be open, honest about your emotions, all while gaining a sense of freedom, control, and hope, is a catalyst for transformation. You don't have to heal alone; there is healing in community.

As a therapist, I routinely recommend support groups for my clients in addition to therapy sessions. Support groups allow survivors another protected space to dig deeper into the many layers of domestic violence. For instance, a standard therapy session is approximately 50 minutes, and support groups on average are 90-120 minutes weekly. You have more time to examine important tenets of domestic violence such as power and control, co-parenting with the abuser, healthy v. unhealthy relationships, legal proceedings, financial literacy, accessing resources, and trauma recovery. Given these barriers, including the lack of community support groups for Black women survivors or groups led by Black women, I co-created an 8-week support group called Bell's Sista Circle: Love, Relationships and Intimacy. The group was facilitated by a Black clinician and researcher that not only had lived domestic violence experiences but studies Black women domestic violence experiences. Bell's Sista Circle is grounded in Bell Hooks, also known as Gloria Jean Watkins, a Black woman author, feminist, social justice advocate known for her writings about Black women, race, and classism. The facilitator and I thought it would be a great way to honor her and her vision while creating a group for Black women healing and recovery. Group topics covered understanding domestic violence, healthy relationships, love and intimacy, balancing boundaries and vulnerability, self care and healing. It was a transformative experience for the group participants. See below:

"I didn't feel alone. It helped me be more vulnerable and made me feel better. I would have never attended a group before-listening to other stories made me feel connected and I could relate to those experiences. I wasn't taught to uplift women, and I appreciate this process seeing sisters support one another. I didn't feel alone and this was a safe space to be honest, genuine and judgment free."

As you can see, support groups can be very enjoyable and rewarding. You hear success stories of survivors overcoming obstacles and triumphing over trauma! You are empowered to try new things while finding your voice. So, if you're on the fence about a support group, I encourage you to give it a try; see how it feels. Also, you don't have to share your story or anything until you are ready to do so. If you're not sure how to find one, contact your local domestic violence shelter or agency. Some agencies may offer free support groups for the community. However, if you're in an area where there aren't many Black people, consider asking the following questions for the facilitator:

- Are you familiar with the complexities of domestic violence experiences for Black women such as racism, discrimination, and disparities among resources?
- What has your experience been like working with Black women survivors?

Faith based support groups

Faith-based support groups play a crucial role in the healing journey for Black women survivors. These groups can provide a safe space where women can draw on their faith as a source of strength and resilience. Grounded in shared spiritual beliefs, these support groups offer not only emotional and psychological assistance but also a community of understanding and solidarity. Through prayer, scripture, and spiritual guidance, you can find comfort and hope, reinforcing your sense of self-worth and assistance to reclaim your identities after experiencing trauma. The support within these groups often extends beyond formal meetings, creating a network of care that sustains women through their recovery.

Also, since we face unique cultural and systemic challenges, faith-based support groups also offer a culturally sensitive approach to healing. These groups acknowledge and address the intersection of race, gender, and spirituality, providing a holistic support system that resonates deeply within our lived experiences. By integrating cultural practices, music, and shared histories, faith-based support groups empower Black women survivors to navigate their healing journey with a sense of belonging, cultural pride, and powerful catalyst for long term recovery, personal growth, helping survivors rebuild their lives with renewed faith and confidence.

Counseling

I wholeheartedly feel that seeking counseling from a licensed mental health professional is critical to your healing journey. I know I am biased, but counselors are essential members of your supportive community. But before I go in depth on the role of counselors in your healing, let me address some common beliefs. You may feel that as long as you are not experiencing physical abuse or never experience it, then you can manage healing on your own. However, emotional abuse, also known as invisible wounds, are more damaging than physical abuse. They are scars that you cannot see, taking a toll on your psychological well-being. Or, perhaps, you may feel that since you are no longer in the relationship and proud of your efforts to leave, you do not need any assistance. Indeed, you should feel proud because leaving is a challenging process; you survived living in a war zone. I celebrate you! But have you checked within yourself and wondered what impact that battle zone has had on your emotional, physical and spiritual well-being?

Does this sound familiar: You don't want to air your dirty laundry or talk to a stranger? But let's reframe it this way: if you had a broken arm, you'd visit a doctor to treat the symptom. Right? If you suffered physical injuries as a result of the abuse….you went to the doctor; so treat your emotional wounds the same as your physical wounds. So think of counseling as an avenue to address the emotional symptoms. We know abuse damages your emotional and mental health, and you need support from a trained, licensed counselor to help you manage the effects of the domestic violence trauma on your mental health. I know you may be saying, you have your mother, sisters, girlfriends, family, church folks; and they are great, but they're not trained to help you understand the extent of the symptoms on your life and recovery journey.

Counselors play an important role in your recovery from domestic violence. A trusted partner that will help you reclaim your voice and restore your autonomy. Also, counselors provide you tools to manage emotions to foster a healthy, positive mindset. In addition, the symptoms can impact your ability to function or engage in day to day activities, such as inability to concentrate at work or sleep due to depression and anxiety. To add to that, a licensed counselor performs an assessment that will include a diagnosis of the symptoms and an individualized treatment plan to reach your wellness goals. For diagnosis, licensed counselors utilized the Diagnostic and Statistical Manual for Mental Disorders (5th) edition also referred to as the DSM. The DSM-V contains descriptions, criteria, and symptoms for mental health disorders. It helps guide the treatment plan and goals. Similarly, physicians utilize a DSM to diagnose a physical or medical symptom. Now, let me address diagnosis, because I know the thought of "diagnosis" causes fears of being misdiagnosed or "labeled", which keep people from seeking counseling. Also, I understand the historical context associated with mistrust of physicians and systemic barriers; these are valid concerns. However, you are in the driver's seat and can ask questions or get a second opinion. Language is so important with diagnosis, as we tend to say "I'm depressed," but you are not depressed, you are a beautiful Black Queen living with depression as a result of experiencing domestic violence. Depression, anxiety, PTSD, or whatever the diagnosis is one part of you and not all of YOU.

Here are my recommendations for seeking assistance from a licensed mental health professional. A LCMHC—Licensed Clinical Mental Health Counselor, LCSW—Licensed Clinical Social Worker, Licensed Psychologist or Licensed Marriage & Family Therapist. Also, try and find a licensed mental health professional that has experience, training and understanding of trauma, complexities of abuse and, if possible, lived experiences of Black women. Keep in mind that it can be difficult to find a mental health professional trained in domestic violence; let alone a Black therapist. There are many reasons, and I want to mention two: 1) The mental health profession is still a white male-dominated profession, and even though we have made improvements, there is still a shortage of Black mental health professionals. For example, the American Psychiatric Association (2021) found that 2% of the 41,000 psychiatrists in the United States are Black and 4% of psychologists are Black, 2) Many mental health professionals don't receive much domestic violence training in their graduate programs, and this can be problematic as counselors may not be aware of domestic violence screening and safety issues during clinical intake assessments.

Also, licensed mental health professionals may not recognize trauma symptoms, resulting in misdiagnosis. In addition, lack of training could result in further victimization. For example, my research found that survivors were revictimized by shelter and social support staff. Finding a licensed mental health professional that gets the Black women experience is like icing on the cake! Representation matters, and a Black woman mental health professional who gets us and sensitive to the dynamics of domestic violence is ideal. However, if you cannot find one; don't lose hope. There are licensed mental health professionals that understand the dynamics of abuse, trauma, and oppression. You may say why is Dr. Brown discussing the pros and cons of counseling – well, I want you to be aware to make an informed decision, advocate for yourself and affirm your feelings. So, with that being said, be open to seeing a White licensed mental health professional; I did and I want to share a glimpse of my experience.

The first counselor I saw during the abuse was a Black female counselor. Even if she wasn't Black, I was still open to working with someone that didn't look like me because I knew I needed at the very least a safe space to discuss the abuse. When I started counseling, I didn't have a plan to leave the relationship; quite frankly, I didn't want to end it. I was confused, afraid and unsure what to do, but that one step forward was a huge step in starting my healing journey. It was so comforting to have a safe, non-judgmental space to discuss the abuse, my childhood and just everything I was feeling. Throughout my healing journey, I've had Black and White licensed counselors. Each counselor prepared me for the next journey. It's like getting what you need in that season in preparation for the next season. I like to think of this as stages: Counseling while still in the abuse and Counseling after the abusive relationship.

Counseling While Still in the Abusive Relationship

When I first started counseling, a lot of sessions focused on my safety, including creating a safety plan and coping tools. For instance, I learned that I could not control my abuser's behavior but had a choice on how to respond to keep myself safe. Also, my safety plan included a list of people I could contact if I was in danger and places I could go for protection. Creating the plan was an eye-opening and overwhelming experience, because 1) I had to think about non-judgmental people I could tell if needed, and 2) safety planning illuminated that domestic violence is really a thing and I'm actually experiencing it; just WOW. While you're in the abuse, a lot of times, you don't think about your safety... just shocked that this happened and praying it doesn't happen again. You're conditioned to think more of the abuser than yourself. If you're interested in more information about safety planning, check out the National Domestic Violence Hotline at www.thehotline.org for an interactive guide to safety planning. I often use this tool with clients, and they find it helpful and empowering.

Something else I learned was the many ways domestic violence can show up such as emotional abuse, manipulation, isolation, spiritual abuse; it wasn't just physical abuse. I was able to connect witnessing domestic violence in my childhood as a relational template for future relationships. However, the dilemma for me was that I grew up seeing healthy and unhealthy behaviors, leaving me confused and staying in the relationship three years after the physical abuse. The physical abuse stopped, but the manipulation continued. He controlled my mind and thoughts so much that he guilted me into thinking that hiding inside a closet whenever his ex-girlfriend came by unexpectedly wasn't as bad as physical abuse. I didn't see then that this was abusive behavior.

But the beauty in this is that every counseling session propelled me forward: I became a little stronger; began to find my voice and challenged his behavior. What about setbacks? Of course, but I failed forward. Meaning, I learned through counseling that leaving an abusive relationship is a process. Research shows it takes a survivor approximately seven attempts before a survivor permanently leaves an abusive partner. There are many reasons:

leaving can be dangerous; once the abuser knows you want to leave, violence can escalate, resulting in death, 2) Cycle of Violence: as mentioned earlier, breaking free from this vicious cycle is difficult; 3) Isolation – you may not have any family or friends for support or anyone that knows about the abuse; 4) Hope for change—you love the abuser and have this hope that things will get better; 5) Children—you stay for the sake of the kids – want a "two parent home" 6) Lack of financial resources—you may not have your own source of income. All of these factors mentioned above—except children—impacted my decision to leave. So, my setbacks were lessons learned; not regrets. The biggest lesson learned during this stage was that the abuser has to acknowledge their problem, take accountability, and make a change. Once I accepted my abuser for who he was, I made the decision to depart the relationship. Without certainty, I could not have made this decision without the assistance of my counselor; I am grateful that season pushed me forward.

Counseling After the Abuse

Once you have left the abusive relationship, you may think everything is over. No more pain, no more abuse, no more walking on eggshells. Sound familiar? However, it is far from over. Leaving an abusive relationship is the start of a new life; a brave move that is the catalyst of your healing recovery. Counseling after the abusive relationship helped me further examine my behavior; in other words: why I was attracted to guys that were not available or emotionally healthy. I learned that if I thought I wasn't good enough, then accepting the bare minimum was okay. For example, I felt it was better to have half a man than no man. Besides, if the guy was not abusive, it was a real plus, in other words, I settled. This took me some time to accept, but made sense to me. An abusive relationship rips apart the fiber of who you are; you are lost, confused, and don't know who you are. You feel ashamed, embarrassed, like Eve in the Garden of Eden. For example, Rachel shared, *"I don't know... I guess I'm really trying to find myself. I really can't tell you anything other than my name and my children's names and ages. I guess it's kind of hard because I don't even know who I am."*

Essentially, you are trying to put yourself back together, and it's very exhausting. Counseling after the abuse helps you develop insight, gain self awareness, and provide tools to make better decisions. It requires a lot of time, work, patience, consistency, self-compassion, and grace. Especially because survivors tend to beat themselves up a lot for what they have experienced; "I should've known better", "I ignored the red flags", "I broke up the family", "I am a failure."

I learned that I couldn't do anything about what I didn't know in the past, but could do something about the present. This is a very HARD concept, but once you accept you are not responsible for the abuse… a huge burden is lifted. I took daily steps, literally one step at a time, as a pathway towards liberation. Therefore, counseling after the abuse is so critical, as you really need a trusted, supportive person that can hold space for you to process what you have experienced and guidance on moving forward. You may be wondering, when do I start? I suggest that you start when you are ready. This is your journey and while it can be challenging to make decisions due to being controlled, you can make this decision on your own terms. I found it helpful to take breaks from therapy throughout my healing journey. For example, after I got out of the relationship, I needed time to regroup. Regrouping for me looked like getting into a rhythm with life after the abuse. I was focused on graduating and life after undergrad studies. I did not jump into another relationship because I was afraid. I was afraid of heartache; repeating the same mistakes. I still thought the abuse was my fault, so I shut myself off from connecting with others. However, when I got into my first relationship after the abusive relationship, I thought it was helpful to seek counseling to discuss what I was experiencing.

For instance, I found myself questioning if he was faithful, wondering what he was doing when we weren't together, repeatedly checking social media posts, being hypervigilant during conflict, just a lot of obsessive thoughts and anxiety. However, I have gained some coping strategies, such as reframing my thoughts to reduce anxiety. So much clarity in this second phase of counseling. A lot of "aha" moments. What was most profound for me was learning about my relational patterns and triggers. As I mentioned earlier, I learned the reason behind selecting men that were not available was because I didn't think I was worthy of a man that was emotionally available and faithful. I was used to chaos and conflict. It all made sense; I witnessed peace and chaos in my childhood. My brain was used to drama; therefore, healthy relationships were abnormal and felt different. I was always prepared for war; literally, a helmet, shield and sword; ready to fight. However, this phase of counseling helped me realize that healthy relationships do exist, and I do not have to be guarded. I learned and am still learning that I am worthy of a loving relationship free of violence. I wholeheartedly believe that. Also, I have made a lot of progress regarding insight about relational patterns. It's a great, liberating experience to connect the dots, and I am at peace with every relationship I have experienced thus far because I have learned what led me to it. No regrets; just lessons learned.

Counseling after the abuse has been very different because I learned ways to heal the trauma in my body and identify and manage triggers. The first phase of counseling focused on safety and provided a lot of CBT tools to reframe my thoughts. However, from my clinical and personal experience CBT does not go deep enough to address triggers - those sudden reasons you feel (panic, fear, sadness) when something reminds you of a past hurt. Another reason is talk therapy occurs in the cerebral cortex, and trauma is stored deep in the brain. As I mentioned in the Trauma chapter, triggers usually come from old emotional wounds or unhealed trauma that live in your body and nervous system, not just your thoughts. I had to learn the connection between my body, mind, and trauma. For example, I have accepted that my brain was protecting itself during the abusive relationship and did not allow myself to feel. I have learned that it is very possible that I disconnected myself in previous relationships after the abuse and never paid attention to my body and how triggers manifested.

This phase of counseling evolves as I evolve. As I mentioned, each season of counseling prepared me for the next journey. I gradually connected the dots and healed the trauma that impacted my body. This looked like learning tools for emotional regulation and reprocessing trauma so that I am less reactive. I do not want to explode on people or be reactive, so I found a trauma therapist to heal the trauma and gain self regulation tools. For instance, I have learned to pay attention to my body when I am triggered and how to calm it. I have developed emotional regulation tools that I did not have during the first phase of counseling. Some of my favorites are deep breaths, box breathing, tapping, and container. Counseling after an abusive relationship is hard, challenging, yet rewarding. I am reclaiming my body; I am more attuned to my body and have a better sense of how to calm it. I am intentional about this journey because 1) I now understand my trauma wounds and how they show up presently, 2) I know that true healing comes from God through therapy, and 3) The past is my present when I do not engage in trauma work. Therefore, I am not asking God for any additional answers; just healing. He is doing that through therapy. My faith sustains me and provides so much hope and optimism. I am enjoying this phase of my life.

Now, you may wonder if you need counseling after the abusive relationship, more than likely, yes. Many of my clients sought my services because they wanted to heal the core issue; understand why they shut down, explosive behavior, tired of walking on eggshells, hypervigilance, etc. If that is you, I encourage you to give counseling a try to heal the inner wounds so you can be free. While everyone has a different experience, healing from an abusive relationship is a journey of self discovery towards freedom. Remember, you do not have to heal alone.

EMDR Counseling

If you are still experiencing triggers, anxiety, symptoms of PTSD, depression or anything previously mentioned, I highly recommend you seek EMDR therapy. EMDR stands for Eye Movement Desensitization Reprocessing, an eight-phase treatment approach, which has been proven to be effective to help people heal from difficult experiences, especially trauma. Think of it as a way to "unstick" your brain from painful memories that keep causing distress.

When something traumatic happens, your brain sometimes struggles to process it fully, leaving you with strong emotions, thoughts, or physical reactions that resurface, even when you don't want them to. EMDR helps your brain process these memories in a healthier way, so they don't feel as overwhelming or disruptive. You also gain tools to self-regulate your physical and emotional reactions to the memory, so that it no longer causes distress. With that in mind, you do not have to retell your abusive story in EMDR therapy, and many survivors find that aspect really helpful. Retelling a trauma story can be triggering to survivors, which makes EMDR an ideal form of healing. Instead, the focus is on what you are feeling in your body and where that sensation shows up in your body.

So, what does it look like? In EMDR sessions, the counselor will identify the target memory, ask the client to identify the worst part of the memory, negative core beliefs associated with memory, and location of distress in the body. Next, the counselor will guide the client to focus on the troubling memory while using techniques like moving your eyes back and forth (often by following their hand or a light) or tapping of your hands. This bilateral stimulation helps your brain naturally work through the memory, making it less painful and more manageable over time. It's a bit like organizing a messy closet—things are still there, but they're stored neatly, so they no longer clutter your mind. The end result is that you still remember the event, but it doesn't hurt anymore or not as bad. And, EMDR is not hypnosis—it's an evidence-based highly successful, trauma-focused psychotherapy for PTSD.

I am EMDR trained and have seen tremendous benefits with my clients. I obtained this training because I noticed my clients had reached an impasse in therapy; essentially, they stopped progressing. They continued to experience triggers; thus, the ethical thing to do was refer them to a trauma therapist so they would become less reactive. After I completed the training, I prayed to God to help me connect with an EMDR-trained therapist. After a four month wait, I began EMDR as a client in 2020. Not only did he answer that prayer, but the bonus was a faith-based EMDR trauma therapist—my therapy sessions started with prayer and ended in prayer! Oh, let me add that she was White; Whew—GOD did THAT!

Brainspotting

Brainspotting is a mind-body approach to healing trauma. It can help you heal from traumatic experiences that you may be blocking out. The core concept of brainspotting is that where you look affects how you feel. As you learned from the trauma chapter, trauma is stored deep in the brain, and brainspotting heals trauma throughout all aspects of the brain. This is done by a trained, licensed counselor in which they utilize a pointer and slowly guide your eyes until it fixes and focuses on a particular point in space, in other words, the brainspot. The designated spot assists in activating, processing, and overcoming mental, emotional pain. I have experienced brainspotting, and it helped me move past an area that I felt stuck.

Whether it is CBT, EMDR, or brainspotting, be intentional about your overall mental and emotional health. More than likely, you will be facing lasting effects of the abuse. This is a normal and natural response after all your body, mind, and spirit has endured. It is emotionally taxing and nobody can heal alone. Consider support from a trained, licensed mental health professional.

In closing, our ancestors have provided the foundation of community. Enslaved people fellowship together to maintain their sanity while living in an oppressive society. Whether they danced, sung, or worshiped—they were together and not alone.

There is a generation of Black girls behind us that need our wisdom and tools for healthy relationships. My tribe has remained solid throughout my healing journey, and I have added more people as I continue to evolve. What I have learned is that I can add people to my tribe that I find safe, nonjudgmental, trustworthy, and supportive to my healing community as I deemed necessary. What remains true is that I wouldn't be where I am today, without God, and a loving affirming community. I am grateful.

Reflection Prompts

1. Identify your community; write down their names. Examine ways you find them supportive or non-supportive.

2. Reflect on a time when you felt supported by a community, whether it was your family, friends, or faith-based group. How did that support impact your healing journey? In what ways did it help you reclaim your sense of self and move forward?

3. Consider the role of community in your life today. How does being surrounded by a supportive group of people contribute to your ongoing healing and personal growth? What steps can you take to strengthen your connections with others, and how might this enhance your overall well-being?

CHAPTER 7. THRIVING AFTER ABUSE

"You became who you needed to be in order to survive, but now it's time to become who you need to be so you can thrive in life."
—Topher Kearby

Thriving after domestic violence is a journey of resilience, self-compassion, and renewal. This chapter delves into the transformative process that survivors undergo as they rebuild their lives, regain their sense of self, and discover new potentials. By exploring personal stories, psychological insights, and practical strategies, I aim to illuminate the path from surviving to thriving. Here, we celebrate the courage it takes to heal and the incredible capacity for growth that lies within every individual who has endured the trauma of domestic violence.

Thriving after abuse encompasses a multifaceted journey of personal growth, healing, and empowerment. It involves reclaiming one's sense of self-worth and autonomy, establishing healthy relationships, and finding joy and purpose in life. Thriving can manifest as emotional stability, where you experience a sense of peace and resilience, and the ability to set and achieve personal goals. It also includes the development of strong support networks, engagement in fulfilling activities, and the courage to envision and pursue a future free from the shadows of past trauma. Ultimately, thriving is about transforming the pain of abuse into a foundation for a vibrant, empowered, and meaningful life.

For me, thriving after abuse means accepting my flaws, my takeaways from past relationships, trusting my decisions, and embracing this new version of me. One of the hardest battles I faced in my healing journey was overcoming self-blame, and the negative belief that I am not good enough. I blamed myself for failing to recognize red flags and choosing partners that were not good for me. As a thriving survivor, I have released what I didn't know then and appreciate the steps I have taken for healing. I have more empathy for that version of me that decided to stay and other choices I made during that time of my life. I now realize I was in survival mode. I did what I needed to do to survive. I honor myself and no longer blame myself for engaging in survival techniques. Also, I am able to quickly reframe negative beliefs such as "I am not worthy" to "I survived domestic violence that made me question my self worth". "My worth is not determined by someone else's harmful behavior to me". This simple but powerful reframe has changed a lot for me. Now, I want you to think of any lingering negative beliefs and the opposite of it. For instance, I am not good enough—I am good enough. Notice what you feel in your body and the positive shift in your attitude.

Another thriving moment for me is accepting that I can be vulnerable with men of romantic interest without explosive arguments. As I mentioned before, vulnerability is a superpower and does not come easy. I was so used to conflict that I sometimes got tense, guarded—essentially prepared for battle whenever I attempted to express my feelings. For example, during a conversation, a friend noticed that I became quiet and posed three questions:

1. Do you have something you want to say?

2. Why are you looking like that?

3. Are you okay?

This was a game changer for me, as I was triggered and had shut down because I didn't have words to articulate what was happening to me. The ironic thing is that an explosive argument never happened, and I later realize it is possible to be vulnerable. I also realize it is possible for someone to be attuned to you and honor your feelings. This experience shed light on two things: choose partners that help heal your wounds versus repeatedly ongoing emotional turmoil and unfulfilling relationships. I deserve a calm love, someone that is a safe space and not stressful. As I have no desire to keep re-experiencing past pain.

Now, I am getting more comfortable and learning to articulate what I want and need without fear of retaliation. I have identified what I need headed into courageous conversations to feel safe. I am trusting myself more and being okay with making mistakes. I embrace all parts of me and recognize I will get triggered as long as I am alive, and not every trigger is meant to harm me. It is okay, and that I have resources. Also, I practice more self-compassion if I jump to conclusions without facts that are rooted in past experiences. I gently tell myself... it's okay... that's an area to keep working on. For instance, when I am triggered during vulnerable conversations, I have statements in my toolbox such as: I am feeling overwhelmed and need a moment. I need to revisit this as I don't want my response driven by emotions.

Another thriving moment is recognizing people, environments that no longer serve me, and how to love myself more by releasing it. Now that can be hard, especially if it is family, but if it doesn't help me move forward, bring peace or help towards my goals, what purpose does it serve? Now, I get it... the old adage... everything has a purpose... but sis, thriving means we have the right to decide whether it's right for us and not based on people's beliefs, family, or whatever. Also, thriving means alignment. For instance, walking away from people that don't match the healed version of me. I deserve relationships that make me feel safe versus walking on eggshells. Aligning with people that are committed to holistic wellness: spiritually, physically, emotionally, and financially. No one is perfect, but I know my worth. Practicing self-love, self-compassion and alignment is a journey, and a vital part of thriving after abuse. I won't always get it right, as perfection does not exist, but I am listening to my body more, trusting myself, and it feels good to honor me.

There are so many thriving moments, but the most important

one for me is healing the relationship with myself. Thriving after abuse is ongoing, and I want to share key steps that I found helpful to foster long-term well-being:

1. Seek Support: Connect with trusted friends, family members, or support groups who can offer emotional support and understanding. Professional counseling or therapy can also provide a safe space to process trauma and develop coping strategies.

2. Ensure Safety: Prioritize personal safety by informing one to two people of your whereabouts when you enter the dating scene and that may include changing phone numbers, securing a safe place to stay, and obtaining legal protections if necessary.

3. Focus on Self-Care: Engage in activities that promote physical, emotional, and mental well-being. This might include exercise, healthy eating, mindfulness practices, and hobbies that bring joy and relaxation. Some of my favorite self-care activities include prayer, meditation, exercise, skating, doing yoga, spending time with family and friends, going to the beach, solo trips, and rest.

4. Set Boundaries: Learn to establish and maintain healthy boundaries in all relationships to protect personal well-being and prevent further abuse. Now, creating boundaries and enforcing them is a journey. Boundaries tell people how to treat you, so if you haven't seen it, you don't know how to enforce it. Be gentle with yourself and take steps to maintain optimal wellness. There is no right or wrong way, but I have found a helpful book titled Set Boundaries, Find Peace by New York Best Seller Times Author Nedra Twabb. I use her book with clients, and they found them very practical.

5. Build Financial Independence: Work towards financial stability through education, job training, or employment opportunities. Financial independence can significantly enhance personal empowerment and security. I went back to school to further my education, and at the time I didn't recognize I was building financial independence. Now, don't get me wrong, I am not that independent woman that says she doesn't need a man; I do. But I don't need a man solely for financial purposes. I believe God created us to be in healthy relationships for his glory. I believe in having a partner that complements me; mutual empathy, respect. Additional ways I have gained financial independence is by taking courses, coaching, furthering my education, and professional networks.

6. Educate Yourself: Understanding the dynamics of abuse and its impacts can help in recognizing patterns and preventing future abusive situations. Educational resources and workshops can be valuable tools. For instance, I attended The National Conference on Domestic Violence for the first time in my career—it was amazing to be in community with like-minded individuals—empowering and invigorating.

7. Engage in Community: Becoming involved in community activities or volunteer work can provide a sense of belonging and purpose, helps to rebuild social connections, and build confidence.

8. Pursue Personal Growth: Set personal goals that foster growth and fulfillment, such as continuing education, developing new skills, or pursuing creative endeavors. For example, I want to renew my spin class certification and retake piano lessons.

9. Practice Patience: Healing is a gradual process, and it's important to be patient with oneself. Celebrate small victories and acknowledge the progress made along the way.

10. Find Empowerment: Embrace the journey of self-discovery and empowerment. Recognize and honor personal strengths and achievements, and cultivate a mindset focused on resilience and hope for the future.

Survivors' Stories of Resilience & Hope

This section is aimed at empowering survivors of domestic violence. Your resilience and strength are a testament to the incredible journey of healing and thriving after abuse, and I believe when survivors share their stories or insights, it helps break the culture of silence, myths, and can be a beacon of hope for others.

The anonymous quotes and insights shared below showcase the diverse and powerful ways in which Black women can rebuild and flourish after domestic violence. They are guided by the following prompts:

1. How have you reclaimed your sense of self worth and autonomy?

2. What strategies or practices have been instrumental in your healing process?

3. Share specific ways you have rebuilt healthy relationships. Romantic relationships?

4. What does thriving after abuse mean to you?

How Have You Reclaimed Your Sense of Self-Worth and Autonomy?

"I have reclaimed my sense of self worth and autonomy through various methods of rediscovering myself. I have engaged in weekly therapy, journaling, daily sermons, reading books, listening to podcasts, and simply doing things that bring me joy. These various methods have reminded me of who I was prior to the abuse, but also of who I have always been meant to be outside of my trauma responses."

"I've reclaimed my self worth and autonomy by accepting it is okay to set boundaries, to have me time, and to give myself grace."

"Learning to set healthy boundaries and stick to them, put myself first, and make choices based solely on what I want and not on the opinions of others."

"This journey has been beautiful yet challenging. There has been great freedom in reclaiming myself. I have found my voice again; no longer sitting in silence and burying my feelings. I discovered the most important love in me."

"It has been extremely helpful having the ability to identify, work through, and communicate my triggers. And I can't say enough about setting boundaries! All of these foundations have allowed me to enter into a healthy romantic relationship and repair old ones. I now only seek out spaces in which I feel safe, loved, and respected. I show up for myself everyday because I am worth it. I am forever grateful for the investment I've made in myself."

"As a survivor of domestic abuse, I can tell you that it has been a long road to recovery. For years, I struggled with trying to figure out why I felt lonely, sad, and depressed. Although I remarried quickly after leaving my abuse, I for years felt like I was just off. I never really felt like myself. My new husband has been wonderful in helping with my recovery. He has always supported any efforts of mine to come to understand myself and was always encouraging me to seek help. It took years, but there came a time when I just knew I had to do something to get better. Just like I found the courage and strength to learn about what abuse does to someone. I decided to get therapy when I did, I learned so much about why I was feeling the shame and guilt that go along with being abused. I delved deep and spent hours reading material related to helping domestic abuse survivors. I spent time doing therapy and yoga, which were wonderful. I finally learned to talk about what happened to me and not feel like it was my fault and, that in itself, was liberating! I have reconnected with old friends. I had built up such a wall, afraid to have relationships because of the many trust issues I had. I am still working on myself; I feel like this is a lifelong journey, but I feel good about the progress I have made."

"I continue on this journey of reclaiming my sense of self worth and autonomy. If I am being completely honest, my sense of self worth and autonomy were low before I entered into an abusive relationship. One might even say that was one of the main reasons or sole reason I entered into an abusive relationship. Of course I didn't realize it at the time."

"In some things, I had a strong sense of conviction particularly at work when I was responsible for a certain area and supervising a group of people that were part of a union. I had to completely rely on my sense of what is right to do and what is not right to do. This sense of what is right to do was cultivated by watching my parents live by this principle and ultimately by my reliance on my Lord and Savior Jesus Christ."

"This sense of what is right to do, based on what the Bible says is right to do, came full circle for me in the beginning of the end of the abusive relationship I was in. You see, after many months of my therapist trying to show me what healthy relationships should look like and me making every excuse for the bad behavior from my partner, I started to read God's word and again after many years of not using God's word as a yardstick, I started to do so. All of a sudden, behavior that I condoned because that is what a Godly wife does, started to look very evil when put against God's standard. All of a sudden, it was not okay for my children to get yelled at for something the adult in their life ought to handle. It was no longer okay to hold my children to a double standard, or continually move the gold post on them."

"As you can see, my faith in Christ plays a significant role in my life and in me regaining self worth and autonomy. I believe it is God who has also used therapy to significantly impact my life. It has been a slow, arduous but necessary journey."

"For about nine years of the fourteen year relationship, I was a stay-at-home mom. Starting a new job after the separation was really challenging and life changing. Coming into the workforce after such a long time and after being in an abusive relationship, I had no confidence and felt like everyone on the job was doing me a favor. I almost always deferred to everyone

else but myself. Slowly, as I was given more responsibility, my confidence started to grow. The more I did well in my tasks, and the more I was bold enough to take on things I had never done before, and do well in them, my self worth grew. As I grew in my job and my responsibility expanded to supervising others, I watched myself hold my own against unfair treatment, I saw myself stand tall and defend what is right to do."

These last four years of healing have seen me try new things that would never have done before. I have tried things without fear of failure. I have had to talk to myself a lot through this process, using my tools such as positive self talk and deep breaths when fear inevitably raises its head and self doubt begins. I have relied entirely on God keeping me and have seen major miracles in my life, including the miracle of charging the heart of this once terrified woman to a woman trying new things, finding new strengths, and loving life.

"After my divorce, I wanted to be in a relationship. I didn't realize it at the time but I felt the need to prove to myself that I was not the reason my marriage ended."

I'm still on the journey to reclaiming my whole self and I'm UNlearning so many "truths."

What Strategies or Practices Have Been Instrumental in Your Healing Process?

"Talk therapy with a therapist and my support village, identifying lessons learned from my past, and looking at my past and present behavior patterns are methods that have been instrumental in my healing process."

"I have placed strong emphasis on my faith and reminding myself of who I am in Christ. I have taken scriptures and utilized

them as words of affirmation to myself. Some examples are "I am fearfully and wonderfully made" and "God knew me before he formed me." These scriptures remind me that nothing has taken my Father by surprise. This empowers me to know that I am worthy of all things that I desire, and I am capable of doing hard things.I also incorporate a healthy lifestyle. I eat healthy (most of the time lol) and workout at least three times a week. Lastly, I give myself lots of grace. I am growing to understand that healing is not a linear process. I give myself space to grieve the things that make me sad, and celebrate the things that bring me joy. One day, one moment at a time."

"Bi-weekly therapy sessions & EMDR sessions—find a therapist that you trust; your family/ friends are not your therapists, but they can be part of your support system! EMDR has helped me so much with reprocessing traumatic events from my past relationship & childhood."

"Daily affirmations—I'm pretty crafty so I made an affirmation jar. I decorated the jar, wrote affirmations on pieces of paper, and placed it on my nightstand. Each day I take one out of the jar, put it in my purse or pants pocket, and read it at various times throughout the day."

"Prayer & meditation—Carving out time in my day to just be present in the moment. Not achieving, working, or doing anything allows me to stay centered and check in with myself."

"Journaling—This is my favorite! This is the space, other than therapy, where I am 100% vulnerable. And on those days when I may have been triggered or feel that I have not made progress in my healing journey, I go back and read old entries to remind myself of just how far I have come."

"Although I am experiencing grief, I'm devoted to doing the work to heal my brokenness. Healing is a non-linear practice and my nervous system has been a constant force in navigating this journey. I'm giving myself grace and patience, celebrating small victories and surrounding myself around folk invested in my uplift. I'm embracing this journey as an opportunity for

reclamation and reflection. Additionally, my therapist is guiding me through this transition by providing tools to help me unpack and understand my discomfort."

Share Specific Ways You Have Rebuilt Healthy Relationships? Romantic Relationships?

"By just putting myself out there & making myself available to make new connections. I love to attend different events in my area (festivals, grand openings, art shows, fashion shows, etc.), which often leads to me meeting and talking to someone new. I met one of my friends at a fashion show this past year and we've built a healthy friendship over the past few months by getting to know each other, being honest, and setting boundaries."

"When I was ready to begin dating again I used the dating app BLK. Before downloading the app, I wrote a list of the type of relationship and partner I wanted. I found the dating apps easier for me because there was less pressure. I could chat with the guys I matched with and if I liked the vibe then we would exchange numbers and set up a date."

"I have learned that NOW is the time to be transparent when communicating with my loved ones instead of internalizing conversations. I've learned to pay attention to detail in my romantic relationship as well as to not project past experiences on my mate, build trust, work on effective communication, allowing myself to be vulnerable, most importantly learning to accept love."

"I have finally gained an understanding of healthy boundaries. I used to think that boundaries were something to be stated to others, and then restated to others when they were crossed. However, I understand that boundaries are all about me, and my love and respect for myself. I have learned to treat myself as the strong yet fragile person that I am. I pay attention to how I feel both physically and emotionally when interacting with certain individuals. I no longer force connections with people who are not good for my overall health. I gravitate towards the

relationships that help me grow, and feel the most loved. I understand the difference between unhealthy and healthy communication. I give people space to be themselves, but also give myself the choice of whether I want to be in a relationship with them. This goes for friends, family, acquaintances, or pretty much anyone that I interact with. I am still rediscovering myself in a romantic relationship. As a starting point, I utilize the same measuring stick for all relationships across the board. I'm learning to discern the "tree" by the "fruit" it produces."

What Does Thriving After Abuse Mean to You?

"Thriving after abuse means Phil 4:13 and Proverbs 3:5-6. It's a deep sense of resilience, peace, freedom, and becoming. I'm becoming what I was purposed to be. Each day is a testament to my personal growth and renewal. I'm finding comfort in my own strength and allowing hope and JOY back into my life. There is no greater agony than bearing an untold story—Maya Angelou

"Thriving after abuse means letting go of the expectation that I have to "get myself back" or wanting to feel like "my old self again" but instead finding who I am now."

"Thriving after abuse means the metamorphosis of being a victim to now living as a VICTOR. Thriving is being FREE to live, love, talk, show emotions, and being vulnerable without struggle and strife."

"Thriving after abuse means that I allow my testimony to help remove the shame and guilt from others who have been through or are going through an abusive situation. It means that I am able to forgive without reconciliation or hatred towards the abusers. It means that I am able to recognize that abusers are broken/unhealed individuals who have made a choice not to heal. Thriving means that I press ahead in faith, with optimism knowing that I have great days in my present and my future. It means being okay with not having everything figured out. It means that I have a toolkit of resources available to me to assist

with my healing journey; and that I utilize these tools daily. It means that I have peace. It means that "I don't play about me."

As you can see thriving after abuse is a profound journey that speaks to the strength, resilience, and beauty within Black women survivors. Moving beyond survival, we reclaim our narratives, find our voices, and embrace our power. Healing becomes an act of self-love and resistance, as we honor the women who came before us and pave the way for those survivors that will come after. In community, we draw on the wisdom and support of each other, reminding ourselves that we are not alone.

Moving Forward

As we come to the completion of this guide, I want you to know how proud I am of your efforts to pour into your healing journey. Taking these steps to prioritize your well-being and reclaim your power is no small feat. Healing is an investment— a commitment to nurturing your mind, body and spirit as you move beyond the pain of the past. Remember, every small step forward is a testament to your resilience and worth. Thriving is not meant to be a solo journey. As you step into this new season, think about how you can create spaces for others to heal alongside you. Start a small support group - gather trusted friends, survivors, or community members for regular check-ins. Share your story when you feel ready, whether in a local forum, community, a podcast or through writing. Your voice, journey, and your leadership have the power to spark change. Take the first step. Healing multiples when we heal together. Finally, I hope you always remember that you deserve a life filled with peace, joy, and the fullness of thriving. You deserve a life free of violence. You are worthy simply because you exist—see yourself as God sees you—radiant in his righteousness. Sis, keep thriving. I am with you.

"Experiencing domestic violence is a point of reference, and each day is a step forward filled with hope, healing and gratitude." —Dr. Shanita Brown

Reflection Prompts

1. What does thriving after abuse mean to me at this stage of my life?

2. What strategies or practices have been instrumental in your healing process?

3. How have you reclaimed your sense of self worth and autonomy?

4. Share specific ways you have rebuilt healthy relationships? Romantic relationships?

5. What dreams, passions or part of myself am I ready to reconnect with now that I am in a new season of healing?

Activity

1. Write a letter to your younger self affirming her worth, strength, resilience and right to be protected and loved.

REFERENCES

1. Brown, S. (2016). Intersections of Race, Spirituality, & Domestic Violence: The Counternarratives of African-American Survivors. (Dissertation). North Carolina State University, Raleigh, NC.

2. Centre Safe. (2009). *Cycle of Violence Infographic.* Retrieved from https://www.centresafe.org.

3. Collins, W., & Moore, S. (2006). Theological and practice issues regarding domestic violence: How can the Black church help victims? *Social Work & Christianity, 33(3)*, 252–267.

4. Costs of Intimate Partner Violence Against Women in the United States (2003). Centers for Disease Control and Prevention, National Centers for Injury Prevention and Control. Atlanta, GA.

5. Crenshaw, K.W. (1995). Mapping the margins: Intersectionality, identity politics, and violence against women of color. In K.W. Crenshaw, N. Gotanda, G. Peller, & K. Thomas (Eds.), *Critical race theory: The key writings that formed the movement.* (pp. 359–383). New York, NY: New Press.

6. Domestic Abuse Intervention Programs (DAIP, 2017). *Power and Control Wheel.* Retrieved from https:www.theduluthmodel.org

7. Herman, J.L. (2015). Trauma and recovery: The aftermath of violence - from domestic abuse to political terror (2nd ed.). Basic Books.

8. Hetling, A., & Zhang, H. (2010). Domestic violence, poverty and social services: Does location matter? *Social Science Quarterly, Special Issue: Inequality and Poverty: American and International Perspectives, 91(5)*, 1144–1163.

9. Leemis, R..W., Friar, N., Khatiwada, S., Chen, M.S., Kfewnow, M., et al., (2016). The National Intimate Partner & Sexual Violence Survey: 2016 Report on Intimate Partner Violence

10. Miles, A. (2002). *Violence in Family: What every Christian needs to know.* Minneapolis, MN: Augsburg Books.

11. Parker, B. (2022). *Bell's Sista Circle: Relationships, Love & Intimacy.*

RESOURCES

1. National Domestic Violence Hotline: 1-800-799-SAFE

    Text START to 88788 for connection to a Hotline advocate

    https://www.thehotline.org/

2. Ujimma - The National Center on Violence Against Women in the Black Community

    www.ujimacommnity.org

3. National Sexual Violence Resource Center

    https://www.nsvrc.org/

4. Battered Women Justice Project

    https://bwjp.org/

5. A Call To Men

    www.acalltomen.org

BIBLIOTHERAPY

There are many amazing books that provide insight, encouragement and practical tools to support your healing journey. Here are a few I recommend.

1. *What Does He Do That? Inside the Minds of Angry & Controlling Men*, by Lundy Bancroft.

2. *Homecoming: Overcoming Fear and Trauma to Reclaim Your Whole, Authentic Self* by Dr. Thema Bryant.

3. *Set Boundaries, Find Peace: A Guide to Reclaiming Yourself* by Nedra Twaab.

4. *The Body Keeps Score: Brain, Mind and Body in the Healing of Trauma* by Bessel Van der Kolk.

ABOUT THE AUTHOR

Dr. Shanita Brown is a Teaching Assistant Professor of Counselor Education at East Carolina University, a Licensed Clinical Mental Health Counselor, trauma specialist and sought out speaker. Dr. Brown has a Doctor of Philosophy in Counseling & Counselor Education from North Carolina State University.

Dr. Brown is the owner of a private practice with over 20 years of clinical experience in the mental health field. Her work has been featured in scholarly articles, podcasts and media outlets such as Checkin with Michelle Williams, *Essence* and *Self Magazine*. Dr. Brown enjoys the beach, exercise and time with family and friends.

You can learn more about Dr. Brown at
www.drshanitabrown.com

www.ingramcontent.com/pod-product-compliance
Lightning Source LLC
Chambersburg PA
CBHW071757120626
46550CB00002B/829